P9-CST-551

The Feminist Mystic

THE FEMINIST MYSTIC

❦ *And Other Essays on Women and Spirituality* ❦

Edited by Mary E. Giles

CROSSROAD · NEW YORK

ACKNOWLEDGMENTS

The essays "The Courage To Be Alone—In and Out of Marriage" and "The Feminine Dimension of Contemplation" first appeared in *Studia Mystica*, Winter 1980. Used with permission.

Excerpt from "Ash Wednesday" reprinted by permission of Faber and Faber Ltd. from COLLECTED POEMS 1909–1962 by T. S. Eliot.

1985

The Crossroad Publishing Company
370 Lexington Avenue, New York, NY 10017

Copyright © 1982 by Mary E. Giles

All rights reserved. No part of this book may be reproduced, stored in a retrieval system, or transmitted, in any form or by any means, electronic, mechanical, photocopying, recording, or otherwise, without the written permission of
The Crossroad Publishing Company.

Printed in the United States of America

Library of Congress Cataloging in Publication Data
Main entry under title:

The Feminist mystic, and other essays on women and
 spirituality.

   1. Women and religion—Addresses, essays, lectures.
I. Giles, Mary E.
HQ1393.F44   305.4   81–22130
ISBN 0–8245–0432–1   AACR2

To
Teresa of Avila
1515–1582

Contents

The Feminist Mystic

Introduction

There are no sure voices to guide us. We listen for them, anxiously, and search the lonely corners of books and churches and, yes, even the minds of friends and teachers, but none echoes the counsel of reassurance for which we yearn. We shake the old order with cries of anger and contempt, demanding its yield of authority and knowledge, but when the words fall, we cover our ears against the shallow ring.

We are a present, suspicious of the past, uncertain of the future. We are the women of solitude, being taught the art of living in and through the Spirit, and it is not easy.

It is not easy precisely because the assured voices of religious and social institutions and traditions which we believe instructed women in the past seem still. What we hear is debate: That women should be priests and ministers; that women should abandon altogether the Christianity of institution and create new models for adoring; that women should reactivate goddess worship.

Debate wearies, especially when clamor from both sides threatens to negate the very reasons and conditions that gave rise to debate in the first place. It requires but little reading and research — and living — to realize that there are valid reasons for women to question our historical place in churches and in light of that history to assess our situation today and attempt a program for the future. Scholars like Rosemary R. Ruether, Georgia Harkness, Joan Morris and Sarah Pomeroy have contributed enormously to our understanding of how women have fared in Christianity and other religions over the centuries. The insights of Letty Russell, Mary Daly, Sheila D. Collins, Margaret Crook and Phyllis Tribble, to mention only a few names, have created new possibilities for theology and inspired hope that the experiences of women may deepen and make more subtle our knowing God.

Granted the value of such inquiry and our exhilaration at discovering that we as women merit study, we may tire, nonetheless, of a debate that appears endless and too often strident and self-serving. I do not propose to end controversy, for in itself it is stimulating and necessary to growth. As to stridency, that is controversy's companion and we must simply acknowledge it as such. I would hope, though, that we could be in accord in one respect: That we might all aspire to perceive the harmony and unity that exceed the limited focus that characterizes debate.

We may not yet hear that harmony, but it is there, silent before the noise of competing voices but never silenced by them. Women who know the solitude of the solitary endeavor are open to it, this music of oneness to which mystics of all times and traditions attend and upon which they play, each one a unique variation. Whether we speak of Teresa of Avila, who lived in sixteenth-century Spain or her near contemporary, the Indian Mirabai, theirs is the calm and strength of living harmonized and centered in the eternal Center, called God by one, Krishna by the other. As women, they knew controversy, of course, but it did not disturb the peace of one whom love refines.

Such women are not creations of pious fancy; they were women who laughed and loved, wept and despaired. Like us, they were women for whom living was a daily encounter with pettiness and bigotry. But they did not submit to discord; the harmony of love prevailed.

There are no sure outer voices to guide us, but there is the sureness of this inner music that every mystic, man and woman, heeds. How each one came to hear and heed the music within is individual narrative, just as the story of each of us must be uniquely ours and no one else's.

There is encouragement and wisdom in the stories of the mystics, as the essays in this collection reveal. In the first essay, "The Feminist Mystic," I show that women mystics in the past, specifically Teresa of Avila and Catherine of Siena, were feminists and as such, appeal to women today. There is no contradiction in the terms "feminist" and "mystic" if we inquire below the surface meaning of the word feminist and allow its deep significance to emerge from the story of the women themselves.

Like the feminist mystic, we strive to be uniquely ourselves. The effort takes us into solitude and aloneness because no one or no thing can substitute for us in the task. But there is a rich precedent for the dark journey in loving as I explain in "Take Back the Night," for the traditon and theology of apophatic mysticism provide and support reasons for our being detached from dependence on human knowledge and human ways of knowing about God. We see that anything less than an immediate encounter with the divine yields inadequate knowledge.

Stripped of dependency on images, concepts and systems that are largely the construct of a male-dominated theology and institution, we are freed to see God as we do rather than according to the sanctioned models of a church. Meinrad Craighead summons us to participate in her unique loving in "Immanent Mother" as she discloses in the marvelous language of the poet her compelling attraction to God the Mother.

Margaret R. Miles picks up the theme of aloneness in "The Courage To Be Alone — In and Out of Marriage," and elaborates it particularly in terms of our relationships with other people. We are inclined, tempted, to demand that relationships bear the burden of defining who we are, but ultimately we must confront the fact that we are alone and in that aloneness discover the challenge and beauty of creating ourselves.

As solitude and aloneness reveal their loveliness, the feminist mystic desires to cultivate its rich potential, and we find that countless women before us have felt a similar longing. Wendy M. Wright in "The Feminine Dimension of Contemplation" probes the transforming process that occurs in and through contemplation. A delicate combining of the insights of modern psychology and traditonal mysticism illumines the inner journey as women may experience and express it.

The feminist mystic, then, is centered in her contemplative aloneness, but she is never lonely. She is eminently and exquisitely social. Women mystics of the past, even those who, like Julian of Norwich, lived in the anchorite mode, were intimate participants in society, and though they may have lived physically apart, they related to others through their bodies in the same ways that we do. As Dorothy H. Donnelly explains in the "The Sexual Mystic: Embodied Spirituality," the feminist mystic must be sexual because she relates, and in relating she employs the body. In making our understanding of "sexual" more discrete, we free ourselves from the dichotomy of body and spirit that has long marred Christian loving and free ourselves to unite with human and divine lover in most profound joy and chaste passion.

Being social, we cannot ignore a world that struggles and suffers. The feminist mystic thrusts outward in social action, as Kathryn Hohlwein discloses through her portrait of Simone Weil, she who was "armed with a burning patience." There is tension in the mystic as she lives within and without, but the tension does not drive her in opposing directions; it is rather the dynamic that makes her visible and knowable to those about her.

Such is the feminist mystic: unique, solitary, contemplative, social, sexual. Words, of course, cannot circumscribe her, nor can they us. But words do lightly touch upon her; they catch the fire of her delight and resonate with the joy of women who may enter the debate but remain ever attentive to the inner desire that sustains and enhances the single note of each voice, gathering and resolving them into the harmony of loving.

Mary E. Giles

CHAPTER 1

The Feminist Mystic

❦ *Mary E. Giles*

By themselves, feminist and mystic are evocative labels. Coexistent, they are sharp potential for polemic. Polemic is surface event, slight indicator of the stuff of living —mystery and love and dark solitude. But polemic can hint at paradox, and in this sense "feminist mystic" goes beyond a call for debate.

Although paradox does not yield to essay as it does to poem, essay can brace the mind to the fact and force of its mystery. So this essay is a bracing of the mind to the paradox that the mystic is feminist. To touch the paradox, I suggest we set aside for now the labels and seek out the spirit of loving, seek out the great lovers who care nothing for polemic, absorbed as they are in the art that recognizes neither boundary nor coexistence. Bright creators, they give birth in love to loving at most unlikely times, times like the fourteenth century when apocalyptic forces assaulted a society weakened in spirit and body and bred desperation and anguish.

That ignominy bred beauty also, a woman of amazing accomplishment, of even more amazing love, a fire that chastened the corrupt and emboldened the weak. Catherine of Siena was this great lover, born in 1347, a woman destined to counsel mighty rulers and bequeath a literary treasure such that six centuries later the Catholic Church would bestow on her the title of doctor.

The family into which Catherine was born was not distinguished, except perhaps by size; she was the twenty-fourth of twenty-five children. Raymond of Capua, her biographer, recounts that her extraordinary spiritual gifts were early apparent. At the age of seven she vowed her virginity to God; at fifteen she cut off her hair to thwart the family's efforts to marry her; at eighteen she received the Dominican habit and began a life of solitude in her room at home. The prayerful solitude lasted for three years, culminating in her mystical espousal to Christ. Then, at the age of twenty-one, love impelled her to external action, and she served the sick and poor with a group of women called the *Mantellate*; affiliated with the Dominican order, they wore habits but lived in their own homes. For the rest of her life Catherine was a living oneness in her public service, prayer, study and spiritual teaching.

As Catherine's reputation for devotion and compassion grew from 1370 to 1374, so did her anxiety about corruption in the Church, and by 1375 she had committed herself to the political arena, persuading the cities of Pisa and Lucca not to join the alliance against the Pope and in the following year traveling to Avignon on behalf of the city of Florence, which Pope Gregory XI had placed under interdict. There she convinced the pope to return the papacy to Rome. In 1377, having returned to Siena, she founded a woman's monastery, and late that same year or early in 1378 she was again in Florence to promote peace between that city-state and Rome. At the behest of Urban VI, successor to Gregory XI, who had died in March of 1378, she went to Rome where, accompanied by many of her disciples, she spent the remainder of her life, struggling to heal the schism and bring peace to Christendom. Physically exhausted, she had to restrict her activities for the Church by the beginning of 1380. Unable to eat or even swallow water, she lived in prayer, herself a living prayer. Catherine of Siena died on April 29, 1380 at the age of thirty-three.

Even so summary an account of Catherine's life as this conveys the image of an extraordinary woman. We do well to remember, however, that deeds alone are mere data of impoverished chroniclers; they reflect but do not contain the loving that impelled the acting and that for us draws the image from the mind into the heart.

We need to emphasize that through her acts Catherine realized herself as *woman*. In refusing to marry, she acted as a woman in response to fourteenth-century womanhood and in so doing created her own being as woman. Marriage was, of course, the obvious state for women at that time, as it had been for centuries. The fact for us to consider is not that she did not marry, but that she chose not to marry. She rejected the state of marriage in order to move independently and uniquely as woman.

The other usual option for women was to enter the convent; this too she refused to do, even though that state might have provided more biological and spiritual freedom than marriage as well as the opportunity to exercise real religious-political power.[1] Rather than accept options that were limited by conventions and expectations, she chose to remain unmarried and live in the seclusion of her room at home. She chose to affiliate herself with a religious group whose members by tradition were widows. Indeed, if we examine her life detail by detail, we will see that she consistently acted in a free manner, creating an atmosphere and style in and through her person that was consonant with *her* needs and desires. Whether she was ministering to the poor or dealing with the papacy, her mode was hers. Listen to her, for example, as she urges Gregory XI in a letter not to heed an anonymous letter he had received that warned him he would be poisoned if he dared return to Rome and remember that hers is the voice of a woman without social prominence or formal schooling:

> And I beg of you, on behalf of Christ crucified, that you not be a timorous child, but manly. Open your mouth, and swallow down the bitter for the sweet. It would not befit your holiness to abandon the milk for the bitterness. I hope by the infinite and inestimable goodness of God, that if you choose He will show favour to both us and to you; and that you will be a firm and stable man, unmoved by any wind or illusion of the devil, or counsel of devil incarnate, but following the will of God and your good desire, and the counsel of the servants of Jesus Christ crucified.[2]

She is no less adamant in tone when she writes to the King of France:

> The other matter is, that you maintain holy and true justice; let it not be ruined, either for self-love or for flatteries, or for any pleasing of men. And do not connive at your officials doing injustice for money, denying right to the poor: but be to the poor a father, a distributor of what God has given you. And seek to have the faults that are found in your kingdom punished and virtue exalted. For all this appertains to the divine justice to do (pp.168–169).

This is the voice of Catherine of Siena, "a powerful and effective woman by anyone's standards."[3]

Abundant in praiseworthy anecdote, biographies of Catherine inspire admiration, but admiration is risky for often it slides into adulation.[4] To some the Catherine of admiring biographies seems too remote for us to consider her a realistic precedent for women today. However, if we listen to Catherine herself in *The Dialogue*, we feel ourselves in the presence of a woman who, like us, was conscious of love pushing her to radical action. Granted the impulse may have been more forceful in her than in many of us and that her response was more intense than ours, still the radical nature of that energy, radical in the total demands it makes upon us, was not exclusive to Catherine.

We know something of the genesis of *The Dialogue* from her biographer, Raymond of Capua:

> So about two years before her death, such a clarity of Truth was revealed to her from heaven that Catherine was constrained to spread it abroad by means of writing, asking her secretaries to stand ready to take down whatever came from her mouth as soon as they noticed that she had gone into ecstasy. Thus in a short time was composed a certain book that contains a dialogue between the soul who asks the Lord four questions, and the Lord himself who replies to the soul, enlightening her with many useful truths.[5]

Catherine had written of the mystical experience alluded to here in a letter to Raymond, written in early October 1377; she probably began the work soon thereafter, completing it before the summons to Rome in November 1378. Catherine, who had not been able to read until she was almost twenty, learned to write "miraculously" in 1378.

The most effective commentary on *The Dialogue* is our own remembrance of loving. *The Dialogue* is the love song of the soul and God, of Catherine and her Beloved. It plunges us into the ecstasy of loving and engages us in the passionate colloquy of lovers whose hearts are one. To approximate the oneness of which Catherine speaks, let us recall moments of feeling so intimately bound in mind, body and emotions to another person that we are conscious of no need or wish to explain and justify the passion. We revel in the moment that exceeds time and exclaim in words that exceed language. We feel ourselves unique lovers, and at the same time uniquely in communion with all loving. We merge in love until there is neither the one nor the other.

Thus joined in desire to her Beloved, Catherine begs to know God ever more profoundly, and because she is His, glowing image, heart and mind His, He confides in her, and His caresses are Truth. Loving in eager patience and bold humility, she feels herself become her Love, and caught and enflamed in Him, she dares speak the Truth that is God. She dares grant the petitions that she herself presents because the flame of desire has destroyed all barrier of self-enclosure and freed her to be Him.

The four petitions she presents are for herself, the reform of the Church, the whole world, and especially peace in Christendom and "for a certain case which had arisen" (p. 26). God's responses to the petitions occasion her magnificent mystical theology.

Let us now listen to Catherine describe the soul as it is about to present the second of the petitions:

> Then that soul stood before the divine majesty deeply joyful and strengthened in her new knowledge. What hope she had found in the divine mercy! What unspeakable love she had experienced! For she had seen how God, in his love and his desire to be merciful to hu-

> mankind in spite of their enmity toward him, had given
> his servants a way to force his goodness and calm his
> wrath. So she was glad and fearless in the face of the
> world's persecution, knowing that God was on her side.
> And the fire of her holy longing grew so strong that she
> would not rest there, but with holy confidence made
> her plea for the whole world (p. 55).

Then Catherine pleads out of the consciousness of the soul:
"Have mercy, eternal God. on your little sheep, good shep-
herd that you are! Do not delay with your mercy for the
world, for already it almost seems that they can no longer survive! Everyone seems bereft of any oneness in charity with
you, eternal Truth, or even with each other: I mean, whatever love they have for each other has no grounding in you"
(p. 55). In the sureness of intimacy, Catherine describes God
and then responds out of the consciousness of her Beloved:
"Then God, like one drunk with love for our good, found a
way to fire up an even greater love and sorrow in that soul. He
showed her with what love he had created us (as we have already begun to tell) and he said: 'See how they all lash out at
me! And I created them with such burning love and gave
them grace and gifts without number—all freely, though I
owed them nothing'" (p. 55). God concludes the response to
the soul by stating that though people sin, they are his creation and he will love them ineffably: "'And so, in spite of
their wickedness, I will be merciful to them because of my
servants, and I will grant what you have asked of me with
such love and sorrow'" (p. 57).

Catherine is no shy adolescent flirting with God. She is out-
rageous lover. She knows her Beloved—that "as the soul
comes to know herself she also knows God better, for she sees
how good he has been to her" and "in the gentle mirror of

God she sees her own dignity" (p. 48). Love empowers Catherine to press her petitions and love empowers her to know her Beloved's responses.

In *The Dialogue* there is the immeasurable, subtle understanding of God in God that is the gift to the impassioned heart, and Catherine, faithful lover, expresses the Truth as she must, in her style, in her images. Her words are the words of lovers: She sings, she rejoices, she creates. Although she wrote *The Dialogue* in prose, her language is poetic—she *expresses* rather than explains and lets image and metaphor be the honored bearers of her gifts of wisdom, gifts from God through Catherine to us. We cannot meet Catherine in her loving if we do not allow ourselves to be opened to the poetry of her prose. Writing and loving are, after all, both creative acts, born in and out of mystery. Whoever sets pen to paper or opens the heart to another person knows the terror of risk but also the deep delight of having the word and gesture of love slip unexpectedly into existence. There is a letting go in both, or rather a being made to let go. The poem is more than—and other than—we had conceived. So is loving. It too exceeds expectation and defies calculation. Creators and lovers, we submit to existence working through us and edge it with our humbled talent.

So Catherine edged her love in language, fashioning as her primary image that of the bridge, here described by her Beloved:

> Before I show you what I want to show you, and what you asked to see, I want to describe the bridge for you. I have told you that it stretches from heaven to earth by reason of my having joined myself with your humanity, which I formed from the earth's clay.
>
> This bridge, my only-begotten Son, has three stairs.

> Two of them he built on the wood of the most holy
> cross, and the third even as he tasted the great bit-
> terness of the gall and vinegar they gave him to drink.
> You will recognize in these three stairs three spiritual
> stages (p. 64).

Feet, heart and mouth are the three stairs on which the soul
mounts to God:

> The first stair is the feet, which symbolize affections.
> For just as the feet carry the body, the affections carry
> the soul. My Son's nailed feet are a stair by which you
> can climb to his side, where you will see revealed his in-
> most heart. For when the soul has climbed up on the
> feet of affection and looked with her mind's eye into my
> Son's opened heart, she begins to feel the love of her
> own heart in his consummate and unspeakable love. . . .
> Then the soul, seeing how tremendously she is loved, is
> herself filled to overflowing with love. So, having
> climbed the second stair, she reaches the third. This is
> his mouth, where she finds peace from the terrible war
> she has had to wage because of her sins (p. 64).

At each stair there is a gift: That the soul is stripped of sin;
that she is dressed in love for virtue; that she tastes peace (p.
65). The bridge itself is the Son, folding God and humanity
into one embrace. The soul approaches God through the
Son, communes with God and is sustained through the Holy
Spirit.

Opening to Catherine's song, we soon hear the unmistak-
able melody of the Trinity, and once awakened to the theme,
we catch and lightly trace its many variations through ideas
and images. There is, for example, threeness in the soul. God
says: "I made the soul after my own image and likeness, giv-

ing her memory, understanding, and will" (p. 103). The three powers of the soul are distinct but not separate, for one lends "a hand to the other" and their unity is such that God "cannot be offended by one without all three offending" him (p. 104). As the Truth is Trinity, so is the image. Speaking of virtues, Catherine sees patience, courage and perseverance rooted in true charity, and elaborating the variation on the three powers of the soul, she describes them as "gathered and united all together and immersed and set afire in me" (p.148). Out of the lyrical variations of images and ideas in threes comes a gathering, or, as in a sonata, a resolution of them into one.

The loving that is Catherine's song is also Trinity. Love joins God and soul, or rather loving, for this affair of hearts is not an event but a growing, a nurturing, a being together. At first the soul's concern is only for herself; fear motivates her and obedience to God is but insurance against eternal condemnation. Even as she begins to fall in love with God, her loving remains mercenary, for now her purpose is to taste the pleasure of being loved. Eventually selfish loving becomes purified, as through God she is transformed into perfect lover who loves only for the sake of loving.

In following the journey of love through three stages we discern the classical mystical path of purgation, illumination and union, though there is not the rigorous sequence that marks a treatise like that by St. John of the Cross. And in the spirit of mystics before her, St. Bernard of Clairvaux and Richard of St. Victor, for example, the three stages are gathered into a fourth wherein are resolved all distinctions in loving and the perfect lover lives actively and contemplatively, loving herself, her neighbor, her Beloved.

The Dialogue is structured in ten parts, which structure is an architectural resolution of the Trinitarian theme. The sections are: Prologue, The Way of Perfection, and Dialogue, which together serve to introduce the total work; The Bridge, Tears and Truth, in which the central ideas of mystical loving are developed; and The Mystic Body of Holy Church, Divine Providence, and Obedience, an elaboration of the theme of divine providence. In the tenth section, the Conclusion, God resumes the content of the book and Catherine praises the Trinity. Her praise is a resolution of the resolving of three into one which is the essence of the entire dialogue:

> O eternal Trinity! O Godhead! That Godhead, your divine nature, gave the price of your Son's blood its value. You, eternal Trinity, are a deep sea: The more I enter you, the more I discover, and the more I discover, the more I seek you. You are insatiable, you in whose depth the soul is sated yet remains always hungry for you, thirsty for you, eternal Trinity, longing to see you with the light in your light (p. 364).

This rendering of Oneness in Three, which is the theme Catherine sings throughout *The Dialogue*, echoes Dante's exquisite lines in the last canto of the *Divine Comedy*:

> *Within the depthless deep and clear existence*
> *of that abyss of light three circles shown—*
> *three in color, one in circumference*

> *the second from the first, rainbow from rainbow;*
> *the third, an exhalation of pure fire*
> *equally breathed forth by the other two.*

> *But oh how much my words miss my conception,*
> *which is itself so far from what I saw*
> *that to call it feeble would be rank deception!*[6]

There is no Virgil to guide us through *The Dialogue*, nor is there the polished order of Dante's world. There is only Love, itself the song and the singer, the journey and the journeyer. There is Love, itself Trinity—the lovers and the dynamic that attracts and nourishes them until they are the dynamic.

Thus love moved Catherine to share her loving and wisdom. She was, they say, a natural teacher, and *The Dialogue* was her book of instruction, second only to the book of her total living. Unique lover, she was unique writer also. For when learned men wrote about God in Latin, Catherine wrote in and through God in Italian. When learned men argued the existence and essence of God from positions anchored in logic, Catherine rode the ship of metaphor in a sea of love, and the Truth swept through her. Whoever would seek the order of Scholastic prose in Catherine will miss profound, coherent understandings, but let the mind cede to the heart, and the passion of her words will illumine the darkness that logic obscures.

So too was Teresa of Avila a great teacher and a great lover. With little more education than Catherine, she nonetheless was adroit and secure in her subject matter, possessed of remarkable teaching skills. She wrote at the urging of her spiritual superiors who realized in her attractive and attracting person the power to guide souls to God.

Teresa de Cepeda y Ahumada was born less than two centuries after Catherine, on March 28, 1515 in the central plateau city of Avila. We do not have to rely on the interpretation of biographers for the facts of her life, for Teresa's first major work was her spiritual autobiography, completed in 1565, some nine years after her final conversion.

The portrait of herself as a young girl is notably different from that of Catherine. Whereas Catherine was committed to loving God from an early age and acted always in fidelity to her love, Teresa was anything but spiritually dedicated. She entered an Augustinian convent at the age of sixteen because her family worried about her frivolous behavior. It seems that she enjoyed long hours with some cousins, and she would keep the conversation "on things that amused them and listen to the stories they told about their childish escapades and crazes, which were anything but edifying."[7] "What was worse," she continues, is that her soul "began to incline to the thing that was the cause of all its trouble" (p. 69). Convent atmosphere was stabilizing, especially the example of a certain nun there, and returning to the good habits of childhood, she began to ponder the state of her immortal soul. Five years later, on November 2, 1536, she entered the Carmelite convent of the Incarnation as a novice, professing in November of the next year.

We must pause in Teresa's narrative to consider the facts, for the simplicity of them in this stark recounting belies an emotional complexity. During the years between 1531 and 1536 Teresa endeavored to resolve the direction her life should take. She considered the two options that since Catherine's day and before had been available to women—marriage or convent. In the eighteen months she spent in the Augustinian convent she weighed the options. She envied the virtues in the religious women around her; still she was "anxious not to be a nun," though at the same time she was "also afraid of marriage" (p. 74). She seemed inclined to the religious life, however, for she states that were she to enter, it would not be in the Augustinian convent where she lived because the "very virtuous practices" which she had heard about appeared to her "altogether excessive" (p. 74). If she did choose to become a nun, she confides, she would enter the convent of the Incarnation where she had a close friend.

As we read the Teresian story, we might remember that the unequivocal commitment of a Catherine of Siena was not common to all women who entered the religious life. It is reasonable to assume that many women became nuns because there were few if any alternatives. Teresa was probably typical of women whose first considerations in selecting a convent were those of personal convenience and pleasure.

At any rate, Teresa was not suddenly enraptured by desire for the religious life, and the factor that finally persuaded her to enter the convent of the Incarnation was far from divine love. She had become so seriously ill that it was necessary for her to leave the convent to convalesce. While recuperating, she visited her uncle Don Pedro, a pious man, given to prayer and spiritual reading, and though she remained only a few days in his company, such was his influence that she began to ponder the state of her soul. Now that illness had demonstrated the tenuousness of life, she feared that if she died she would go to hell. Though she still did not want to be a nun, fear made religious life more appealing, and she admits that it was "the best and safest state" (p. 75). Fearful, she wrestled with the decision for months, and when ultimately she determined to enter the convent, it was a decision inspired "by servile fear more than by God" (p. 75).

Here let us recall the early stage of loving that Catherine describes in *The Dialogue*, when fear motivates the soul. Even though Teresa was twenty-one years old when she entered the Incarnation, she was but a novice in loving. By that same age Catherine had experienced mystical espousal and in the flame of charity was ministering to others.

Fear was not the sole motivation in Teresa's decision to become a nun. As a sixteenth-century Spanish woman, she was beholden to honor, both as social code and personal dynamic. Once she made her decision, she was determined to tell her father, which, she explains, was tantamount to taking the habit, "for my word of honor meant so much to me that I doubt if any reason would have sufficed to turn me back from a thing when I had once said I would do it" (p. 76). Her father never gave his consent, and her anguish over entering without his permission was such that "it seemed to me as if every bone in my body were being wrenched asunder" (p. 77).

Impelled by fear and honor to become a nun, Teresa had not the solace of love to ease the passage from family to convent. There was, she confesses, "no love of God to subdue my love for my father and kinsfolk" (p. 77), nor was there comfort from anyone else, for "all thought I had acted out of sheer desire" (p. 77).

Teresa professed in 1537. A year later she was again gravely ill, this time helpless for more than eight months following an attack of catalepsy in 1539. She was an invalid until late in 1541, and the effects of paralysis were with her on and off until 1554. Teresa's suffering was emotional as well as physical. During the three months she was at Becedas undergoing "the greatest trials, for the treatment was more drastic than my constitution could stand" (p. 87), she became friends with a certain priest who had been scandalously involved with a local woman for seven years. Teresa set out to convert him. She succeeded, but in the process she fell in love with him, though "she would not at that time have done anything which she believed to be a mortal sin" (p. 87).[8] It is interesting to note that after she left Becedas and returned to the Incarnation, her health worsened and she had a cataleptic fit on August 15, 1539 that left her unconscious for four days, during which time she was pronounced dead and a grave readied for her corpse.

In 1543 her father died, yet another emotional shock, for he had been a powerful figure in her life, and she in turn had helped him progress in prayer. Then, too, there was the severe spiritual suffering of a woman whose vanity had not disappeared behind the veil but rather had taken different shape. She admits that she always sought to please others and win approval. She was pleased when others praised her patience during illness and lauded her piety and prayer. But Teresa was uneasy in such praise, for she recognized the little progress she had in fact made in prayer as well as the hypocrisy of a nun who counseled others to pray while herself refraining from the practice.

Her spiritual distress deepened in the years from 1536 to 1555 as she realized ever more acutely the emptiness of her inner life. She writes: "On the one hand, God was calling me. On the other, I was following the world. All the things of God gave me great pleasure, yet I was tied and bound to those of the world. It seemed as if I wanted to reconcile these two contradictory things, so completely opposed to one another — the life of the spirit and the pleasures and joys and pastimes of the senses" (p. 105). She spent "nearly twenty years on that stormy sea, often falling in this way and each time rising again, but to little purpose, as I would only fall once more" (p. 108). How like Augustine in the *Confessions* she sounds as she cries: "I can testify that this is one of the most grievous kinds of life which I think can be imagined, for I had neither any joy in God nor any pleasure in the world" (p. 109).

By now Teresa was forty years old. She had been living for twenty years a resolution wrought out of fear and supported by honor. Unlike Catherine, who had created for herself a mode of living consonant with her loving, Teresa had accepted the model of her times so as to avoid condemnation and recrimination. Catherine's course was radical, free and creative whereas Teresa's was conservative and constrained. The first was born from within; the second was imposed from without. Catherine's life was brief but intense and uniquely hers. At the age when Catherine died, Teresa was still laboring to respond to and create herself. In her fortieth year the struggle erupted and was resolved, resolved by grace:

> It happened that, entering the oratory one day, I saw an image which had been procured for a certain festival that was observed in the house and had been taken there to be kept for that purpose. It represented Christ sorely wounded; and so conducive was it to devotion that when I looked at it I was deeply moved to see Him thus, so well did it picture what He suffered for us. So great was my distress when I thought how ill I had repaid Him for those wounds that I felt as it my heart were breaking, and I threw myself down beside Him, shedding floods of tears and begging Him to give me strength once and for all so that I might not offend Him (p. 115).

With this gift of tears, Teresa experienced a radical commitment to God and moved decisively to claim her own direction. Suddenly this woman, who by her own admission had always been concerned about pleasing other people, especially male family members and confessors,[9] took her life into her own hands and with or without permission from superiors, in matters of prayer and reform of the Carmelite order made her own decisions. No longer was she bound by behavior that was "right" or "honorable" or "pleasing." Clearly the reform movement she launched was not right in the minds of the opposition; clearly the establishment of a new convent without "provision" in the city of Avila was not pleasing to its citizenry; clearly it was not "honorable" for a woman to be traveling about Spain as she was to do and carry on spiritual friendship with men. But Teresa was loving God, and what she did out of this love was right, honorable and pleasing.

From her fortieth year until death at sixty-eight she lived with a fervor and creativity equal to Catherine's, reforming the Carmelite order, journeying about Spain to found and administer seventeen monasteries, counseling the princely in Church and state, and writing her masterpieces of mystical literature, *The Interior Castle* (1577) and *The Way of Perfection* (1579). In addition to these, her writings include the *Life*, the *Foundations*, an account of the founding of the monasteries, the *Exclamations of the Soul to God*, poetry, and hundreds of letters.

The swiftness with which Teresa moved after her "conversion" does not imply that she suffered no further distress, for she did. She was, for example, very much aware that as a woman she was ill educated in comparison with the learned men whose counsel she sought and who were to seek hers. After the conversion, when God was leading her firmly in prayer, Teresa underwent months of spiritual tribulation at the hands of confessors who could not understand her soul. In chapter 23 of the autobiography, when she resumes speaking of her life after the chapters on mystical theology, and refers to it as "another and new life" (p. 219), her primary topic is the need for spiritual direction. On the one hand she was afraid to approach learned men because she did not think herself "worthy to speak to them or strong enough to obey them" (p. 221). On the other, she realized that even though some directors were exceptionally learned, they were unable to help her because they lacked experiential understanding of the soul's communion with God. Her ambiguity is reflected in her contradictory advice to her nuns—that they should seek spiritual counsel because they were, after all, ignorant and weak women, but at the same time they were to remain silent about their experiences lest they be misunderstood and ill advised.

Even though Teresa did not always have guidance in prayer from spiritually wise confessors, she continued to pray, for the light within was strong enough to withstand ignorance without. Confused about some understanding God was giving to her and others were endeavoring to clarify for her, she would suddenly be given "a completely clear understanding of the whole thing" (p. 137) by God.

Reflecting on her difficulties with confessors, she recommends in *The Interior Castle* to her sisters that if they were counseled to scorn visions, as she had been, they were not to accept the advice.[10] The authority of the heart overrides that of the mind—even when the heart is a woman's and the mind a man's!

Teresa's advice may seem startling in light of the suspicion with which the Church of her day looked upon those who claimed for themselves supernatural experiences like visions and locutions. But she was daring because she was true to herself, to her loving. The truth within was tested through adversity and realized in action through the years following the conversion, years marked by the Teresian determination we hear so much about. Indeed she does state repeatedly that she determined to do such and such, but hers was a determination imposed not by the mind but the heart. It was determination fired in love—it was loving.

Catherine and Teresa ultimately are similar in the intense loving out of which flow actions outrageously defiant of convention. If I have lingered over the details of Teresa's long struggle to a "new life," it is because most of us can identify with the fact that it took so long for her to "find herself." Somehow the fact of struggle endears her to us.

Catherine and Teresa are also similar in their being writers, untrained but writers nonetheless, and of a stature that is quite simply mind-boggling. Neither woman considered herself a writer in any professional sense; Catherine did not even learn to write until shortly before composing *The Dialogue*, and Teresa squeezed out time for her writing from a schedule so busy that often she was left with only late night hours for the task. She wrote rapidly, as if inspired, with little time for revision.

By the time Teresa was writing, use of the vernacular for ascetic and mystical literature was fairly common. By the end of the fifteenth century many such treatises had been translated into Spanish, and in the second half of the sixteenth century, when Teresa was writing, the volume of spiritual literature was monumental. Much of it, however, was of poor literary quality. In fact, among the numerous religious prose writers, only Teresa and Fray Luis de Granada are considered first-rate stylists whose works are valuable for their literary merit as well as their spiritual teaching. Every student of Spanish literature will encounter Teresa's name among the literary luminaries of Spain's Golden Age, which dates from approximately 1500 to 1680.

There has been a great deal written about the originality of Teresa's style, much of it given over to identifying and analyzing similarities between her prose and that of mystical theologians like Francisco de Osuna. Osuna's *Third Spiritual Alphabet* is the obvious choice for comparison since by her own admission she knew it intimately.[11] We cannot ascertain the exact nature and extent of Osuna's influence on Teresa, but stylistic similarities certainly indicate that he might have been a source for imagery and theology, especially the theology of the experience of recollection in prayer. An example of an image that has intrigued scholars is the hedgehog retracting into itself, an image that both Osuna and Teresa employ to express the soul's being recollected in prayer. In the Fourth Mansion of *The Interior Castle* Teresa says that people being recollected are gradually "retiring into themselves," like "a hedgehog or a tortoise withdrawing into itself" (p. 87). Osuna's image appears in the fourth chapter of the sixth treatise of the *Third Spiritual Alphabet*: "Compare the recollected person with the hedgehog who contracts his body and retreats into himself without concern for anything outside."[12]

Did Teresa consciously imitate the image? Was the image alive in the oral tradition? Was there a common literary source for both writers? Given the available data, we cannot answer these questions, nor need we in order to appreciate the beauty of Teresa's prose.

The commonsensical approach is to assess Teresa as a writer in terms of differences rather than similarities, letting them yield her originality. Consider, for example, how differently Teresa and Osuna employ Biblical allusions. Osuna resorts to extensive enumeration of Biblical references in order to emphasize a point, a technique favored among rhetoricians,[13] whereas Teresa uses one or perhaps two allusions to express hers. In the following passage Osuna employs fourteen references (marked by * and identified in note fourteen) to underscore the need to guard the heart against sensuality:

> The wise man says our eyes are to scrutinize the roads
> so the heart does not go astray, and elsewhere he commands us to watch the tongue that the heart not lie.*

The prophet Isaias asserts that whoever stands vigil over his hands will be fortunate, for thus the heart does no evil,* and in another place we are told to guard our mouths so the heart does not taste our gossiping.* Another passage admonishes us to guard our feet lest the heart fall;* Saint Paul tells us to guard our body in chastity so that the heart is not sullied;* and Moses says we are to fortify our souls with virtue so that the heart is not condemned with it.* If we are ordered to observe God's holidays,* it is so that our hearts may enjoy some quiet and repose; if to guard justice,* it is so that our hearts will be governed well. If it is commanded to respect the law,* that is so our hearts may not experience evil; if it is to guard knowledge,* it is so that our hearts be wise and God's heart delight with them according to what he says.* If we are admonished to guard prudence, it is so that our hearts be governed wisely and know how to rule others; to keep innocence,* it is so that our hearts be without malice. If ordered to guard penance* it is to tame our hearts; and if ordered to keep clemency,* it is so that our hearts may be soft and pious.[14]

Now let us listen to Teresa explaining that if God leads us through locutions, we cannot dismiss them:

When the locutions come from God there is no such remedy, for the Spirit Himself, as He speaks, inhibits all other thought and compels attention to what He says. So I really think (and I believe this to be true) that it would be easier for someone with excellent hearing not to hear a person who spoke in a very loud voice, because he might simply pay no heed and occupy his thought and understanding with something else. In the case of which we are speaking, however, that is impossible. We have no ears which we can stop nor have we the power

> to refrain from thought; we can only think of what is
> being said; for He who was able, at the request of Josue
> (I think it was), to make the sun stand still,* can still
> the faculties and all the interior part of the soul in such
> a way that the soul becomes fully aware that another
> Lord, greater than itself, is governing that Castle and
> renders Him the greatest devotion and humility. So it
> cannot do other than listen: it has no other choice (p.
> 147).

Teresa's one reference (Josh. 10: 12-13) is gracefully integrated into the passage so as to emphasize the greater point she is making whereas Osuna's references become the point itself. Although Osuna does not always employ references in this labored manner, the passage is not atypical of his writing; excessive repetition like this never appears in Teresa's writing.

Teresa's prose is immediately appealing because her language is familiar and direct. The image drawn from life about her, the forceful exclamation of love, the practical bit of advice, even the tendency to drop momentarily one idea so as to knit in another—these are the charm of a writer who in loving breathes the word as effortlessly as air.

I hesitate to describe Teresa's prose with specific adjectives for fear my own interpretation will be limiting. Rereading recently a well-known study on Teresa, I was stunned by the repeated use of the words "virile" and "virility" to describe her writing.[15] Undoubtedly the author intended the words in a positive sense, to express the strength and incisiveness of her language, but the implication for a woman reading them today is not favorable. It is true that Teresa, like Catherine, exhorted other Christians to "manly" behavior in their spiritual journey, but they were reflecting cultural biases that are not necessarily our today. There has been an unfortunate tendency among Spanish scholars to label the prose of their women writers as "masculine" if it is terse and sinewy.[16] Let us just say that Teresa's prose is direct, concise, strong. It is also ornate, rambling, conversational, emotional, etc. It is, finally, just hers!

Teresa, like Catherine, did not rely on literary precedent for a form and style that would be appropriate to mystical literature. Each woman found quite unexpectedly the voice that was singularly hers in imagery, phrasing and tone. The fact that these women had not been educated in universities might have been an advantage for they did not have to overcome the learned art of writing academic prose. (Teresa was very self-conscious about her lack of education, and she often cautions her readers against thinking she was a scholar or theologian.) When we consider the originality of both Teresa and Catherine as writers, our wonder is twofold: First, there is the wonder that these women could write so masterfully without academic discipline; second, we wonder whether the absence of training was not in effect freeing.

* * *

With Catherine and Teresa we are in the presence of women who in the spirit of counsel that Teresa gave her sisters in *The Interior Castle* did what they really could do.[17] The advice is simple enough, but its implications are profound, especially when we realize that for Teresa the search for what was really hers to do was so arduous. The counsel implies that there is something unique for each of us to do, a *quehacer vital* as Ortega y Gasset would call it centuries later, a vital something to do which is our unique response to the creative urge within and which is indeed essential to life.

Both Catherine and Teresa were conscious of the inner impulse, and they responded to it as *women*. When Catherine refused marriage and convent, creating for herself a model of living that was compatible with her inner needs and nourishing of her inner desire, and when Teresa defied male confessors and social and religious tradition to journey in prayer and build a new contemplative order, they did so as women who had discovered within the freedom and strength to move ahead in darkness.

I have spoken of Teresa and Catherine as great lovers and of love as the dynamic of their lives. To live and to love and to create are one. In living, loving and creating we move in mystery, alert to possibility, bereft of model from the past and without hint of one to come. In the absence of model we experience absolute freedom, and in freedom, risk, responsibility and the joy of being opened to whatever the moment may bring forth in us.

Catherine and Teresa were free, joyous, loving and creative, alive in and through their being women. As such they were feminists. The love, creativity, life that are one, they *adored*, expressing that adoration in the passionate word and gesture of Divine Love. As such they were mystics.

Women today are being awakened through a diversity of experience to the inner desire to live, to love, to create. According to the model of Teresa and Catherine, who are models that honor no model, there is no formula for our awakening to uniqueness or for the response to that awakening. If we attempt to pattern the specifics of our living after them, or any other person, we violate our very being. Any adaptation, whether to creed, structure or person, is violation of our being, and attempts at such adapting are failures whose feeble claim to success is that the fact itself of failure may reveal the futility of the attempt.

No creed, no structure, no person, no relationship, nor any combination thereof can provide us identity. If I, a married woman with children, resolved to live out my life in strict conformity with, say, a rule designed for celibate monks, others would quite rightly ridicule or pity my shortsightedness. My efforts, however, might not be viewed so lightly if they were to realize literally the political platform of a contemporary feminist organization. Then supporters of my resolve might applaud the effort as an act of "good faith"; but if in so doing we placed greater importance on my serving the creed than on its serving me, we would all be guilty of self-violation.

We must circle institutions as carefully as we do the ideas and manifestos that support them. Women with religious concerns are assessing from many points of view, including historical, theological and cultural, the institutions through which we have sought to define ourselves as spiritual beings. The problem is that institutions transmit an identity we are supposed to assume. From the silent, and now not-so-silent, struggle to conform to preordained standards in marriage, convent and profession has issued a bitterness and anguish we cannot estimate.

As feminists we should be especially cautious about efforts by women to circumscribe our condition as women and draw us together in "sisterhood." Even though feminist writers envision "sisterhood" as being free from the hierarchical and authoritarian constraints that are said to characterize traditional, male-dominated societies, I maintain that a collective is still a group, and in any group there is structure, hidden or otherwise, different perhaps from those of past and present societies, but nonetheless present. In practice today organizations that call themselves feminist have their own dynamics, which can be as limiting as those of so-called patriarchal groups.

But our response to still-born freedom should not be vindictive or convention-bound. Sex without marriage, a priesthood of women, goddess worship — these are not adequate responses in and of themselves; they are only known options through which *some* women *may* be awakened to themselves. A change of rules is no guarantee of freedom. To gain entry into priesthood for a Catholic woman or to worship "her" rather than "him" may be mere substitution of one pattern for another. It is not the specifics of a model that impose limitations but rather the fact of a model being imposed, and the only person who can know whether or not she is being made to conform to a pattern or is creating her own, which may or may not have precedent, is the woman herself. And there is no prescription for knowing this. It is a knowing born out of experience, happening very early to some, like Catherine of Siena, who when we first meet her through the data of history, is already awakened spiritually, and to others, like Teresa, relatively late in life.

We may be more apt to recognize the perils to freedom that are in institutions than those in human relationships, but the latter are all the more insidious for being less evident. We live in a time and society that supposedly values human relationship — a claim affirmed by the fashion of reading psychology marketed in "how-to" books. Groups and institutes of every ilk spring up to answer every question and minister to every need concerning psyche, body and bonding. There is temporary value in all of this, just as there was some help for Teresa from her spiritual counselors and friends. Ultimately, however, Teresa had to be weaned from dependency on other people so that she could hear unimpeded the voice within.[18] So too must we heed the inner impulse, even if it is discomforting to parent, husband, child, mentor, adviser. It is one thing to comprehend intellectually the admonition to guard ourselves "from the idols" (1 John 5:21) and the statement that "He who loves father or mother more than me is not worthy of me; and he who loves son or daughter more than me is not worthy of me" (Matt. 10:37), but it is quite another to admit to ourselves that we have allowed a loved one to do our living for us, to stand between us and God. Breaking the idol, particularly when the idol is husband or priest, may scandalize church and family, but scandal we can survive; murder we cannot.

There is no such commodity, then, as identity, nor in our journey of living and loving are there any shortcuts. Categories and labels that beckon with the security of ready-made identity lead to disillusionment, their only worth that they may sharpen our instinct for the dark path.

Once darkness overtakes us, we see the labels for what they are—mocked lanterns—and ourselves the authors of the mockery as we evade mystery by arranging experience into events and masking its essential mystery as problem, polemic and contradiction.

If we limit our use and interpretation of language to the level of understanding that is the problem, the polemic, the contradiction, then we will not see the paradox and mystery of living that words can lightly mediate. The conjunction of "feminist" and "mystic" on one level is an example of how language can catch at subtlety of meaning, a subtlety that evades the grosser net of labeling. We have seen that, although Catherine and Teresa were not trained professionally in the art of writing, they did write, and wrote so beautifully that professionals rank them as first-rate writers. If I say

"They were writers but they were not writers," my statement at first blush is contradictory, but given what we know about the women and their writing, there is in it a hint of the paradox that though they were not writers in the professional sense of the word, they were indeed writers. Let us now rephrase the statement: "They wrote though they were not writers." Substituting the verb for the noun in the first clause and changing the "but" to "though" eliminates the harshness of direct opposition and frees the act of writing from the definition or category that is implicit in the word "writer." This change of wording, slight though it may be, modifies and magnifies the meaning of the statement.

Let us work similarly with two more sets of statements about Catherine and Teresa before returning to the word "feminist." The first set is: "They were rebels but they were not rebels"; "They rebelled though they were not rebels." We know that both women refused to be constrained by the social and religious standards of their day, and to the extent that they acted decisively against such limits they did indeed rebel. But their rebellion did not make of them outcasts from institutions. Quite to the contrary, they remained within the Catholic Church while at the same time creating for that institution possibilities that enhanced its own vision of itself. As in the preceding set of statements, the shift here from noun to verb in the first clause effects a change of meaning whereby the act of rebelling is greater than the condition of being a rebel.

In the second set of statements a similar change and deepening of meaning occurs as we shift from "They were theologians but they were not theologians" to "They theologized though they were not theologians." Here we meet the paradoxical fact that they lacked university education in theology but nonetheless taught eloquently of God.

In each of these three sets the contradiction of the first statement, which the direct opposition of parallel constructions (noun versus noun) realizes, cedes to a stronger suggestion of paradox as the change of noun to verb and of conjunction yields greater subtlety of meaning. Perhaps we could visualize the two clauses of the statements as circles. In the first statement each clause with the noun is a circle of comparable size and potential; the "but" is the energy that drives them in opposite directions and holds them in tense balance. In the second statement the circle that represents the verb is enlarged and circumscribes the second circle of the noun. The smaller circle is stationary while the large one revolves around it.

Employing the verb instead of the noun in the first clause is significant. The verb *expresses* doing while the noun *names* a condition or quality. The first is dynamic; the second is static. Through the verb we evoke process, whereas the noun is our effort to distill the process, to halt it, as it were. Women theologians today, as well as men, are emphasizing the verb rather than the noun precisely because it conveys process instead of condition; there is a marked tendency, for instance, to refer to *be-ing* rather than *being*.[19]

With respect to "feminist," it is clear that we cannot move with it as we could with "writer," "rebel" and "theologian." Feminist is an adjective that we employ as both adjective and noun, as in "Teresa is feminist" and "Teresa is a feminist," but there is no verb related to feminist. To "feminize," after all, means "to make effeminate." So we can say that "Teresa is a feminist but she is not a feminist," but we cannot form the second statement of the set as we did in the preceding examples because there is no verb. It seems ironic that feminism, as a contemporary movement that stresses the verb for reasons just clarified, does not itself have a verb to express its own feminist moving. The lack of verb may be constraining, for without the verb to express creative and loving acting such as we have seen expressed through Catherine and Teresa, there may be a tendency to interpret feminist and feminism in terms of condition, the condition of a group or person or theory, and condition, as we have seen, is static.

In order to glimpse the paradox that "feminist mystic" points to, we need to remember that "feminist" is not merely a condition; feminist refers to "unique moving," the unique moving of women like Catherine of Siena and Teresa of Avila that defies the description of label or casual association. Were Catherine and Teresa feminists? Of course they were; the woman mystic *has* to be feminist. For the feminist mystic is she whose flame of Loving sears the edges of life, which edges are only feeble constructs of the human mind anyway. She is bright living in the darkness of Love, the solitary heart, alone but not lonely, she whom we recognize and in whom we recognize ourselves by the clear absoluteness of moving uniquely. She is, and we are, greater than whatever we or others might conceive of and label as ourselves. For we are ourselves paradox, mystery, born and being born out of Mystery Itself.

NOTES

1. Among the many studies that treat the political power of women in convents, see *The Lady Was A Bishop* by Joan Morris (New York: Macmillan, 1973).

2. *Saint Catherine of Siena As Seen in Her Letters*, trans. and ed. Vida D. Scudder (New York: E. P. Dutton & Co., 1906), p. 185. Subsequent excerpts from Catherine's letters are from this edition.

3. Eleanor McLaughlin, "Women, Power and the Pursuit of Holiness in Medieval Christianity" in *Women of Spirit*, ed. Rosemary Ruether and Eleanor McLaughlin (New York: Simon and Schuster, 1979), p. 117.

4. Two examples of such adulatory biography are: Jeanette Eaton, *The Flame: Saint Catherine of Siena* (New York and London: Harper & Brothers, 1931) and C. M. Antony, *Saint Catherine of Siena: Her Life and Times* (London: Burns & Oates, 1916).

5. Catherine of Siena, *The Dialogue*, trans. Suzanne Noffke, O.P. (New York: Paulist Press, 1980), p. 12. All further references to *The Dialogue* are to this edition. I am further indebted to the translator and editor of this edition for the description of the structure of *The Dialogue*.

6. Dante Alighieri, *The Paradiso*, trans. John Ciardi (New York: A Mentor Book, New American Library, 1970), p. 364.

7. *The Life of Teresa of Jesus: The Autobiography of St. Teresa of Avila*, trans. E. Allison Peers (Garden City, New York: Doubleday & Company, Inc., Image Books, 1960), p. 69. All references to the *Life* are to this edition.

8. For an excellent study of this episode from a psychological and spiritual point of view, see the article "A Psycho-Spiritual History of Teresa of Avila: A Woman's Perspective" by Catherine Romano in *Western Spirituality: Historical Roots, Ecumenical Routes,* ed. Matthew Fox (Notre Dame: Fides/Claretian, 1979).

9. For an analysis of Teresa's relationship with men in general, see the article by Catherine Romano mentioned in note 8.

10. St. Teresa of Avila, *The Interior Castle*, trans. E. Allison Peers (Garden City, New York: Doubleday & Company, Inc., Image Books, 1961), pp. 183-184. All references to *The Interior Castle* are to this edition.

11. "On the way there, I stopped at the house of this uncle of mine, which, as I have said, was on the road, and he gave me a book called *Third Alphabet*, which treats of the Prayer of Recollection." This passage is from the *Life*, p. 80.

12. Francisco de Osuna, *The Third Spiritual Alphabet*, trans. Mary E. Giles (New York: Paulist Press, 1981).

13. The following study analyzes this technique among others in a famous Spanish work from the end of the fifteenth century: A.D. Deyermond, *The Petrarchan Sources of "La Celestina"* (Oxford University Press, 1961). Cervantes would use the technique to comic advantage in *Don Quijote de la Mancha*.

14. The references are: Prov. 21:23; Isa. 56:2; Prov. 16:26; Ecclus. 4:17; I Tim. 5:22; Deut. 4:9; Lev. 19:3, 31, Lev. 26:2, Lev.23:37-38, 44; Prov. 3:1; Ecclus. 21:12; Prov. 19:2; Mal. 2:7; Ps 36:37; Prov. 23:13-14; Prov. 11:19).

15. See the study by E. Allison Peers, *Mother of Carmel: A Portrait of St. Teresa of Jesus* (Wilton, Connecticut: Morehouse-Barlow Co., Inc., 1944).

16. Emilia Pardo Bazán is one such writer whose style was often characterized as virile and masculine. She is one of the outstanding Spanish novelists of the late nineteenth century and early twentieth century, and though her writing was strong and sometimes economical, it was also lyrical and richly descriptive.

17. In the Seventh Mansion of *The Interior Castle* Teresa says: "By your doing things which you really can do, His Majesty will know that you would like to do many more, and thus He will reward you exactly as if you had won many souls for Him" (p. 233).

18. See the article by Catherine Romano.

19. For a good discussion of the importance of language, see Mary Daly's *Beyond God the Father: Toward a Philosophy of Women's Liberation* (Boston: Beacon Press, 1973). Matthew Fox in *A Spirituality Named Compassion and the Healing of the Global Village, Humpty Dumpty and Us* also stresses the dynamic thrust of the verb.

CHAPTER 2

"Take Back the Night"
🍎 *Mary E. Giles*

A mong feminists "Take back the night" is a call to political action for women to assert the right to go out at night without fear of injury and violation. For the feminist mystic "Take back the night" is a summons to reclaim our spiritual heritage and enjoy a freedom from fear that at once includes and exceeds the physical and psychological dimensions implicit in the political slogan. In taking back the night feminists do not intend to deprive others of their right to the night, nor do feminist mystics make claims that would impoverish anyone else. We only claim a night that is the spiritual birthright of every person, irrespective of sex or profession, a night that is ours but that for want of adequate commentary from the point of view of women today may seem the exclusive property and experience of theologians and cloistered religious.

The night we would reclaim is the "dark night," the precious, painful dark night through which countless women and men over the centuries have been illumined and transformed in divine loving. We know that the darkness has attracted women as far back as the first centuries of Christianity when women joined the gnostic sect in large part because its emphasis on personal revelation and dark unknowing freed them from institutional restrictions. In her incisive account of Christian gnosticism[1] Elaine Pagels relates how women were drawn to gnosticism with its stress on personal revelation and a knowing that exceeded the bounds and authority of hierarchy and theology and explains the unfortunate consequences for women of the dispute between gnostic and orthodox Christians over the exercise of power. Orthodox Christianity maintained that power resided in apostolic succession, but the gnostics, who were suspicious of institutional power, held to the supremacy of personal revelation. Since apostolic succession was male, women were effectively barred from power in Christianity as the orthodox group gained ascendancy; and by the end of the fourth century, when the Roman-inspired organization of the orthodox group was the Christian church, the secondary position of women in Christianity was settled.

Although gnosticism submitted to a more skillfully organized opponent, its spirit did not die but endured splendidly, if somewhat obscurely at times, in the lives and writings of Christianity's apophatic mystics. The word "apophatic" is from the Greek *phatos*, which means "revealing or sharing feelings" and the prefix *apo-*, which signifies "away from." The related word *apophasis* means "denial." The prefix *cata-* carries the meaning of "akin to" and joined to *phatos* produces *cataphatic*. Whereas the cataphatic mystic comes to know God by affirming the divine throughout the created order and ultimating rejoicing that God is all this . . . and more, the apophatic mystic renounces the possibility of knowing God through creation except insofar as God is neither this nor that. On beholding the budding rose, for example, the cataphatic mystic exclaims that God is this . . . and more, but the apophatic mystic in crying "God is this" pauses and adds "but not this." While the cataphatic mystic journeys in light on the "and more," the apophatic goes forth in darkness on the "but not."

Although at first glance the negative way of apophatic mysticism seems unrewarding, its tradition is fruitful, nourished by Christianity's most eminent mystical theologians. One of its first exponents was Dionysius the Areopagite (sixth century) who in his slender treatise counsels us to "leave behind the senses and the operations of the intellect, and all things sensible and intellectual, and all things in the world of being and non-being" so that we may arise "by unknowing, towards the union, as far as is attainable, with Him Who transcends all being and all knowledge."[2]

The fourteenth century was a spring flowering of apophatic mysticism. That marvel of a mystic, Meister Eckhart, in sermon and discourse touched the still nothingness dear to Zen Buddhists and honored the darkness that begets loving: "For all the truth the authorities ever learned by their own intelligence and understanding, or ever shall learn up to the last of days, they never got the least part of the knowledge that is in the core [of the soul]." And, he continues, "Let it be called ignorance or want of knowledge, still it has more in it than all wisdom and all knowledge without it, for this outward ignorance lures and draws you away from things you know about and even from yourself."[3] While an English contemporary advises us in *The Cloud of Unknowing* to "smite upon that thick cloud of unknowing with a sharp dart of longing love,"[4] another Rhineland mystic, John Ruysbroeck, writes passionately: "In the abyss of this darkness, in which the loving spirit has died to itself, there begin the manifestation of God and eternal life. For in this darkness there shines and is born an incomprehensible Light, which is the Son of God, in Whom we behold eternal life." Through love of God he says that we are "dead to ourselves, and have gone forth in loving immersion into Waylessness and Darkness."[5]

Apophatic mysticism again burst into radiant bloom in sixteenth-century Spain when that dear friend of Teresa's, St. John of the Cross, sang of dark loving in exquisite poetry, and in careful prose elaborated the arduous process of knowing through unknowing. Viewing St. John of the Cross, or some other theologian of apophatic mysticism, from our vantage point today, whether that be inside or outside a religious tradition, our first inclination may be to denounce the literature as esoteric, at best reserved for those living a cloistered life and directed to one aspect of their lives — prayer.

To appreciate the significance of this literature for us today, we must first dispel the faulty understanding that prayer is an isolated act, a something that we indulge in at our convenience, a bit of ourselves. Perhaps it is the frenetic pace of our society as well as our dependence on chronological rather than psychological time that so enfeebles our vision and understanding that we seriously talk about our "sex lives," our "professional lives," our "prayer lives." Of all the "lives" into which we fragment ourselves, the one we label prayer is most likely the tiniest.

If we are to approach mystical literature and specifically the experience of the dark night, which I claim is our spiritual birthright and of value for us, then we must cast out all notion of the divided self and make of that tiny fragment labeled prayer our total being. Rather than speak of our "prayer life," let us think and speak of ourselves as prayer, or in the language of verbs which is significant for the feminists, as praying.

Acknowledged masterpieces of apophatic mysticism, the writings of St. John of the Cross are a reliable entry into dark knowing, and especially in the two-part treatise, *Ascent of Mount Carmel* and *Dark Night of the Soul*,[6] his treatment of the mystical way is incomparable in precision of language and clarity of insight. The image that informs the journey of unknowing is the night, and though John was not the first to employ the night image, his elaborate and delicate rendering is indisputably original. Although the night is one, there can be distinguished degrees of darkness that indicate the progressive darkening of our total being as we travel therein.

The general orientation is away from what and how we know toward that which is unknown. We are progressively detached from the known and knowable, over which we have some control, until, against all our efforts and in spite of them, we are left suspended over the abyss between the known of the past and the unknown of the future. John calls those moments when we understand the process the active night, while the passive night is the lengthier and more painful time when we are being made to endure separation without understanding what is happening to us. A further division that helps us comprehend the process is that between senses and spirit, which division reflects the Scholastic theology and psychology that John inherited and skillfully employed.

The division between active and passive accounts for the two-part structure of the treatise, for the *Ascent of Mount Carmel* is an exposition of the dark journey in terms of the soul's awareness of what is occurring within and her active participation in the process of detachment, whereas the *Dark Night* treats how and why the soul is being made to let go of the known.

Given this distinction between active and passive in terms of consciousness, we can certainly understand that the *Ascent* would be easier reading. We are able to understand the process because she who is on the journey is aware of it, can understand it, and consequently can direct it at least to some degree; and with John's clear reasoning we understand how and why the soul must be denied dependency on knowing God through the senses, emotions and higher faculties of understanding, memory and will. Even if we do not subscribe to the Scholastic psychology of the soul that was John's road map for the journey, we can nevertheless discern and appreciate the truth of his insight that unless the total being that we are is engaged in the process, we cannot become and be spiritually alive.

The *Dark Night* does not allow for intellectual speculation and discussion. It demands the attention of the heart, and though it may be exclusive to state, as mystical writers do, that experience alone can verify the truth of their words, it is fair to say that until we ourselves are drawn into the dark fire that burns away all attachment to the known, we cannot "see" from a within that is without a without the loving that the soul is having to endure. Lack of experience may prevent both theologian and director as well as spiritual novice from realizing that the wisdom John imparts in the short *Dark Night* surpasses the language at his disposal. Even though he may formulate understandings in what appear to be neat categories, they are mere constructs of his mind. As such they are as much to be taken away from our understanding as the classifications of natural and supernatural understandings, which he meticulously describes and upon which he adamantly warns us not to rely as depositories of divine knowledge. Just as his concepts and images must be subject to the

cleansing fire of dark knowing, so too can they yield to inter-
preters of another time, another place, a task that is ours to
assume inasmuch as the people to whom John directed his
counsel were living out their love for God in circumstances far
different from those of most of us. John was writing primarily
for men and women enclosed in monasteries for whom the
gestures and language of prayer were formally structured,
but the majority of us are vigorous participants in a secular
society for whom prayer cannot be a formalized activity to occupy certain hours of the day.

Prayer, of course, is not simply a formal, recitative act,
though there is and was in John's time widespread belief that
such constituted the totality of prayer. Clearly John wrote his
treatises for people who practiced prayer in this rudimentary
form but desired to nourish it into something that would be
their total self.

Here, then, we return to the idea that prayer/praying is
the person herself, which idea is fundamental to John's mystical theology and our present interpretation of it. When John,
for example, treats a particular consciousness that is the transition from meditation to contemplation, he marks it by three
signs that serve to test if the transition is real, that is, given by
God, or imagined and self-induced.[7] The first sign is that we
can no longer meditate or reason with the imagination nor
can we take pleasure in it. The second is the realization that
we do not desire to meditate or enjoy any particular objects,
exterior or interior. And the third is that we desire to be alone
and simply rest attentive to God. Elsewhere he provides three
signs by which to discern if one is experiencing detachment:
1) We find no pleasure or consolation in things of God and
things created; 2) We carefully think on God but derive no
pleasure and believe we are backsliding; and 3) We can no

longer meditate.[8] From these two sets of signs from the *Ascent* and *Dark Night* in general let us now extrapolate principles that are consonant with the subtle understanding of prayer/praying as our being in its totality and that will enable us to discern how the dark night is being experienced by women today.

I have drawn six principles from John's two-part treatise, and although they are not the only possible extrapolations, nor are they meant to be a definitive statement on the process of unknowing, they may illumine the *nature* of the dark night, the specifics of which are necessarily knowable only to the individual undergoing it, and even to her, only obscurely. The six principles we will examine in light of our experiences as women are: 1) That we be stripped of all illusion of knowing God; 2) That the stripping be against our will; 3) That we be suspended between two worlds; 4) That we struggle to the point of helplessness; 5) That we suffer acutely throughout all of our being; and 6) That we love and desire God ever more keenly.

Because the first principle treats of unknowing and as such is fundamental to the entire treatise and consequently to the other principles, it seems appropriate to preface any discussion of it with a brief explanation of modes of knowing and the kinds of knowledge they yield. A helpful distinction in this respect is between the magician who seeks to control the forces of nature and the mystic who submits to its mysteries. Whereas the magician views life as a composite of problems to be solved and powers to be manipulated, the mystic realizes that life is mystery and therefore cannot be reduced to knowable, hence manageable, components. Arrogance rules the magician; humility graces the mystic.

We may not recognize the lure of magic, but in all of us is a bit of the magician who would persuade us that we really can know God in the church theology and rituals we analyze and attend, in the child, friend, lover whose physical and emotional needs we respond to out of our own, in the natural world we study and the art we scrutinize for form and theme. Whether we are too uncaring or foolish to check the premise that the divine can be known adequately through the human or whether timidity allows authority to do the checking for us, the fact is that we are inclined to relate to God as we do to creature and creation—emotionally estranged and yet intimately dependent one on the other.

According to the mode of knowing that the magician employs, we collect data about people, ideas, values, institutions and the divine in a procedure that puts us in what is known as a subject-object relationship, wherein as subjects we are the center of a universe that has all the objects we would dominate with the intellect in orbit about us.[9] In this process of *knowing about* objects, the intellect is a buffer between the center of our being and the center of being of the other, and the assumption, stated or implied, is that what the mind is able to understand it can control.

When we rely on the intellect to know about people, events and values, we are prisoners of our necessarily limited experience and biased understandings. When we extend this inadequate kind of knowing to God, depending on the knowledge that religious dogma, rituals and symbols convey, it is all too common for the intellectual adherence, which is called belief, to become the primary goal, thus confining our knowing to what we understand with the intellect and obscuring the subtle truth that the symbol was originally meant to express but not contain.

There is, however, a second kind of knowing that occurs

when the subject-object structure breaks down and the intellect submits to the heart, yielding a knowledge so delicate that it cannot be bound by any terms and that thus is seen by the human intellect as dark and confused.[10] In this knowing we are centered in the center of the other with whom or which we relate, and our knowledge is greater than and other than what we could explain or even suggest in word or gesture. In religious situations the symbol, ritual and dogma reveal but do not reduce their mystery, and we encounter the divine heart to heart, a naked encounter wherein exists no illusion whatsoever that we know and control God with the intellect. At this subtle level belief is transformed into faith and knowing about God is transformed into knowing/loving God, an immediate meeting that depends in no way on constructs of the mind.

In the *Ascent* and *Dark Night* John describes and explains the process whereby the soul is gradually stripped of all illusion that she knows, hence controls, God. Knowledge of God that comes through the senses is held in the imagination and categorized by the mind and necessarily rises out of sensual, emotional, imagined and intellectual experience, all of which must be stripped away until the soul is left trembling in dark confusion. The soul must be so detached from knowing about God through symbol, ritual, concept, social and religious institutions and human relationships that she is left without a scrap of assurance that she knows/controls God.[11]

John's Scholastic exposition of the process of unknowing gives the impression that progressive detachment from increasingly discrete modes and content of knowing is orderly, but for the person enduring darkness there is little neatness, and for those who endeavor to understand the process from outside, the only constant is that the ultimate and most severely painful detaching from knowing will occur in that aspect of our being where we are most deeply entrenched in the illusion of knowing God. If, for example, the intellect governs my life to the point of directing relationships with others, then the night will be most painful as the support of the intellect is removed, leaving me bereft of the concepts of God that once mediated the divine and served the illusion of being in control.

In the case of Teresa of Avila we can discern two principal modes of knowing that had to be stripped away, the first of which was that of human mediator. Having relied for some twenty years in convent life on male confessors, she was greatly distressed when in prayer she was given understandings through visions and locutions that her spiritual directors later contradicted and advised her to disregard. The struggle to reconcile human and divine authority and understandings finally was resolved when her Beloved told her, "'Be not distressed, for I will give thee a living Book.'"[12] She who had known God primarily through the authority of a male-dominated church was being made to walk in the solitude of dark loving.

For Teresa the process of detachment and breaking of the illusion of control did not culminate in the transition from the natural mode of human mediator to the supernatural one of vision and locution, for even the knowledge that came to her in this second, discrete mode had to be stripped away so that she could stand alone and free in her loving. That the supernatural experiences caused her grief as well as delight is apparent from the account in the sixth mansions of her *Interior Castle*, which reveals that the encounter with God through ecstasy and trance often left her physically exhausted and in pain. And she writes with admitted relief in the seventh mansions that such experiences no longer beset her and that she lived now constantly aware of her divine Lover being present to her:

> This Presence is not of course always realized so fully —
> I mean so clearly — as it is when it first comes, or on cer-
> tain other occasions when God grants the soul this con-
> solation; if it were, it would be impossible for the soul to
> think of anything else, or even to live among men. But
> although the light which accompanies it may not be so
> clear, the soul is always aware that it is experiencing
> this companionship. We might compare the soul to a
> person who is with others in a very bright room; and
> then suppose that the shutters are closed so that the
> people are all in darkness. The light by which they can
> be seen has been taken away, and, until it comes back,
> we shall be unable to see them, yet we are none the less
> aware that they are there.[13]

It is possible that Teresa described the sixth mansions in more detail than the others because in the knowing that she experienced therein was the greater peril of believing herself the holder of special powers and even the author of them. It is precisely because the supernatural mode of knowing can so quickly and insidiously fuel the illusion of control and self-sufficiency that mystical writers adamantly emphasize the need to attribute to it and its yield no special importance.[14]

In considering ways in which Christianity has encouraged women to know and love God, we see from convention and theology that in her customary role of wife and mother she has been conditioned to see God through and in her husband and children. We need not review two thousand years of Christian theology and culture to substantiate the observation that in practice and theory the husband has been the primary mediator of the divine, and as spiritually perceptive writers caution, that which is primary gains primacy. The mediator too easily becomes confused with that which is mediated.

We see social and marriage roles changing, but there still exists strong support for the opinion that the wife is to her husband as man is to God, an opinion which was reiterated only a few years ago by no less an illustrious theologian than Karl Barth, who in the following passage strains to reconcile equality before God with the idea of natural order in which woman, B, is second to man, A:

> A precedes B, and B follows A. Order means succession. It means preceeding and following. It means super- and sub-ordination. But when we say this we utter the very dangerous words which are unavoidable if we are to describe what is at issue in the being and fellowship of man and woman. Let us proceed at once to the very necessary explanation. When it is a question of the true order which God the Creator has established, succession, and therefore precedence and following, super- and sub-ordination, does not mean any inner inequality between those who stand in this succession and are subject to this order. It does indeed reveal their inequality. But it does not do so without immediately confirming their equality. In so far as it demands subjection and obedience, it affects equally all whom it concerns.[15]

The mature woman for Barth is she "who knows and takes her proper place, not in relation to man but in relation to the order" (p. 257). And this order, we might repeat, places women in a subordinate position.

The Christian church in its theology, complex of symbols

and images, and rituals, all of which are largely the work of men, has long fostered the attitude that, although men and women are equal before God, in the created order the male is superior. Feminist theologians and historians are capably demonstrating the theological vulnerability of this position and the profoundly damaging effects it has had on the church and human relationships; and in the sad litany of such effects we ought not overlook the seminal damage, that to the spiritual loving between a woman and God.[16]

It will not be easy to convince men or women that we must let go of and be made to let go of our dependency on human lovers if we are to enjoy divine loving, which bears in us the fruit of human compassion. Meeting God mediately through the male is, after all, secure, comfortable and supportive of the illusion that in knowing about God through men we are knowing and loving God adequately.

But when we settle for mediate loving, we join countless Christian women who live a security that is bound for failure, for eventually, as St. John of the Cross sings beautifully in his poem, "The Dark Night," the only real security is the dark, solitary journey:

> *Secure, in more than night,*
> *close hid and up the stair a secret way*
> *(O windfall of delight!)*
> *in the night, in feigned array*
> *as all my home in a deep slumber lay.*[17]

To be content with knowing about God through family and institutions violates our spiritual freedom, for if we see God only through the human, we risk seeing only the human. When St. John the Apostle advises us to guard against the idols (I John

5:21), he does not mean statues of pagan gods but rather the real idol of excessive attachment to a person, institution, idea, symbol, ritual, an attachment such that the human and the particular are for us the goal and as such our god.

The theology and tradition of female subservience that has caused women to make idols of their husbands and families and suffer consequent spiritual deprivation has also adversely affected women outside of marriage. Catholic nuns, for example, have often idolized the structure of convent and the order of priesthood. Any woman, in effect, who relates intimately with another person, male or female, flirts with idolatry unless her loving is transformed into selfless compassion.

In the exposition of the signs that mark entry into contemplation and passive purgation as well as through all the *Dark Night* there is implicit the second of our six principles, that the stripping of illusion of control through knowing is against our will. The word "involuntary" is an obvious choice of adjective to describe the consciousness of being acted on by forces out of our control, but it does not convey with sufficient strength the fact that not only do we not will the dark night into existence but our wish is that the experience not be. That the dark night is, in spite of our wishes, is the fundamental fact to be met and endured.[18]

However much we may read about the dark night, we are never prepared for it, for if we were, the experience we would call dark night would not be that. It may happen that one has read and intellectualized the spiritual journey as set forth by St. John of the Cross, and perhaps even memorized the signs of entry into passive purgation and contemplation, but what the intellectual journeyer cannot yet know is that darkness is not restricted to the times reserved for formal prayer. It will envelop all of her at all times; thus, while she may be pondering the state of her "prayer life" and assessing its progress on the basis of the signs, the dark night that is to be *her* ordeal, and no one else's, may be moving undetected over her.

Because the dark night must be individual, we cannot and dare not establish its specifics for any one person, but we can state that regardless of the particular terms, its effects will be to force us to acknowledge that we are not in control. If at any time we believe that we are undergoing the dark night and take some comfort in that on the basis of what we have learned from counsel and reading—that what seems negative in this ordeal is spiritually beneficial—then we have yet to experience the total darkness wherein the transformation in loving occurs unknown to us.[19] Only afterward, in the light of transformed loving, can we look back and sigh, "Ah yes, I have been in the night."

Certainly, then, we cannot plan our dark night, nor can we even know we are undergoing it, for to know that is to be in partial control. All we know is that every notion of well-being and security is being destroyed, and our total self, not just what we erroneously call our "sexual self" or "prayer self" or "professional self," but our total self is being ravaged by doubt, despair and disillusion.[20]

I have mentioned already that Teresa suffered because she felt out of control, that her reading and spiritual counsel had not prepared her for the visions and other supernatural events through which God made love to her and rendered her powerless. She suffered because the experiences were unexpected and unplanned and, more importantly, because in her confusion and doubt, as well as that of spiritual directors who on the basis of their limited understanding sought vainly to guide her, she did not want to endure the supernatural.[21] She did not understand what was occuring to her, nor did her confessors, and she was as helpless to deny this way of God's loving as she was to summon it. To the spiritual adolescent Teresa's account of this period in her life may be entertaining reading, for there is admittedly something exotic and romantic in the image of a woman caught up in ecstasy, but romanticism wears thin on the spiritual journey and she who lives expectant of the visions that characterized Teresa's growing will surely be disillusioned.

Although we may understand the fact that the dark night occurs unexpectedly and beyond our control, we cannot avoid expectancy in our lives. No matter how sharply we may remind ourselves not to plan in loving, there is the planner in all of us, and we will make our little agendas, consciously or unconsciously, until such time as in the desire not to be expectant expectancy itself is met and endured. And just as we cannot journey darkly without encountering expectancy, so we cannot arrange the time and place of that meeting.

Women today, especially we who live outside of a religious community and desire to grow spiritually, know how difficult it is to find directors with personal experience of the mystical way who are sensitive to the needs and desires unique to women. This difficulty may account for the great appeal of Teresa and her writings. Reading Teresa's mystical literature can benefit us enormously if we avoid, to the extent that we can, comparing her experiences to ours so closely that we schedule spiritual events to happen to us when and as they did to her.

Most of us live the so-called secular life, in or out of marriage, usually deeply committed to at least one other person. Our dark night will have to affect us profoundly in these human relationships. Let us imagine the sense of loss, disillusionment and anguish that would beset a married woman

who learned of her husband's infidelity. The realization
would happen to her, and in spite of her most anguished efforts to dispel it, its truth would persist. Or let us imagine a
Catholic nun who has lived faithful to church teaching for
many years only to realize suddenly that the mass is an empty
ritual and she is party to the exploitation of herself and her
sisters in an institution that reserves for men its honors and
sacramental powers. The particulars of such situations vary,
but if they are sufficient to cause familiar ways of seeing and
knowing ourselves and the world to die, then their nature is
one. In these situations the usual reaction is disbelief and
denial, which then impels us to seek solutions to what we
would like to view as a problem. Only when we *have* to accept
the fact that what we confront is not a problem — a wrong to
be righted or a circumstance to be adjusted — do we encounter the awful truth that life is beyond our control.

In situations such as I have described our total being is dev-
astated. The faltering commitment to marriage or convent
does not occupy our attention from nine to ten in the morning; it preoccupies us totally — all of the time. Activities may
temporarily dull the edge of awareness, but they cannot wear
it away, for once awareness is born, it grows through us unre-
lentingly and everything and everyone around is affected in
the process. We necessarily see life differently as a result of
the ordeal and other persons relating to us will necessarily respond differently to us.[22]

Just as Teresa endured her ordeal in her own way, so each
of us is destined to suffer uniquely. Mystical literature and
spiritual director can offer general counsel, but they cannot
dictate the specifics of our course or provide a substitute for
suffering. The woman imprisoned in the pain of unwanted
divorce may well be journeying in her own dark night even

though mystical literature does not describe it in her terms, and her confusion will be confounded if her spiritual counselors, like Teresa's, press her to deny what is being done to and through her. Because Christian women by convention have been conditioned to accept greater responsibility for the survival of their marriage, it is not surprising that in face of divorce, which a woman may vigorously oppose, she will flagellate herself with feelings of guilt and remorse.

These remarks are not advocacy of breaking commitments, marital or otherwise, or of rebellion against institutions, but they are a strong statement on the *nature* of the dark night. In being made to accept the fact that we do not control life, which is to say God, we are affected here and now, in the most intimate aspects of our living, and this ordeal is so consuming that it cannot not violate the people and values we cherish most.

The foregoing description of the dark night experience implies that it is a process rather than an isolated happening, though an event may trigger our awareness that something unplanned is occurring. For one who is accustomed to praying mentally, the ability to focus the mind may be too startling to go unnoticed, just as the news of a husband's infidelity cannot be ignored. But other times entry into the dark night is too subtle to catch our attention, and an emotional commitment or cherished belief may have been quietly slipping away long before we awaken to the fact.

When awareness breaks through the surface of routine and self-confidence, we know that we are engaged in a life-and-death struggle, the outcome of which is unknowable. Unable to see or control the outcome, we are tempted to look back and cling frantically to a receding past, but the firmer our grasp, the more severe the pain.[23] Just as in prayer we strain to imagine and think, only to discover time and again that the mind refuses to obey, so in personal relationships we yearn for old intimacies, but in ourselves and others meet a stranger. We cannot see that out of this alienation is being born an intimacy far deeper and more delicate than that which we know or imagine, an intimacy that will reveal to us the heart of being itself.

For us who are suspended between the old and new, there is no comfort, as Teresa so movingly and succinctly expressed when she described herself as crucified between heaven and earth.[24] Like Teresa, we realize in the ordeal that there is no going back, not even on the crutches of memory, nor can we depend on hope which only generates a future out of yesterday's images.[25]

So we strain forward in the night bereft of comfort in remembrance of the past and without hope for the future. Whether it is a marriage that is crumbling against our wishes and in spite of our efforts or some other situation equally devastating to our well-being, we respond by scrambling after the falling pieces, endeavoring to reassemble them in the old pattern or at least rearrange them in a similar one. Both efforts fail, for something new and unknown is in the making, which cannot be denied and which surpasses the sum of the pieces at hand.

In a darkness that honors neither past nor future, we can do nothing but struggle with what we do know. In a failing marriage we must work as never before to revitalize the relationship; in a weakening belief in church and dogma, we must work as never before to appreciate their truth and beauty. We must grapple with and through the known if it is to be discovered to us that our real enemy is the desire to know and control life, which pushes us to depend upon the known and knowable.

It is characteristic of our struggle that, like a battle which has two contending forces, it is dichotomized, between alternatives like to divorce or not, to leave the religious life or stay, to attend or not attend mass. If we do consider a third way, it is usually a mere compromise of alternatives fashioned out of past and present experiences.

In our dark struggle counsel from other people, even those professionally trained, ultimately is of no avail, for their counsel is born from experience that by nature is limited, like ours. Yet we can extend the boundaries of human understanding through counsel and, most importantly, we can test the honesty of our endeavor. It is not sufficient to accept the ordeal meekly or respond to it halfheartedly. We must be brought through "kicking and screaming" if we are to be brought through at all, and for that reason we must exhaust conventional resources, even if this means consulting a minister or priest who admonishes us to return to our old ways and act according to sanctioned models. We cannot know if the models are truly inauthentic for us unless we genuinely test them, and that requires going further and working more strenuously than we ever thought possible.

As the limitations of our knowledge and ability to know become increasingly and painfully apparent, we note a corresponding weakening of will and resolve. So long as the illusion of knowing/controlling braces us, it is relatively easy to make resolutions and follow through on them, but in the dark night determination wanes. In prayer we may resolve to meditate only to realize that we cannot, or we may determine one day to end a love affair and the next day be unable even to consider that an option. The resolve of today is tomorrow's vacillation.

Failure of will refers to the resolutions we consciously make rather than the deep inner current of desire that enables us to struggle at all. Were that desire to fail, we would fall victim to killing apathy.

As our ability to act resolutely weakens, frustration and despair intensify, for we do not wish to admit that we are ir-resolute, nor do we heed the cajoling and recriminations of friends and counselors who remind us of our duties and re-sponsibilities. We are being made to endure in a way that causes our entire being to suffer—emotionally, physically, mentally. We are being detached from the illusion of control and opened up to true loving, and for the price of loss of all sense of well-being there is being purchased for us the awful awareness of being totally and irremediably helpless.

This price we call suffering, and it occupies much of John's attention in the *Dark Night*. Newcomers to John's theology often blanch at the mention of so much pain and suffering, and it is true that he elaborates the anguish of the dark night; but it is also true that this pain is real and unavoidable and if we are serious about spiritual growth, then we cannot gloss over the fact of its existence.[26] No amount of pious breast-beating will dispel suffering. The dark night is to be endured, and to endure means to suffer. Heroism and heroics, by the way, have no place in the inner arena, for she who is enduring is passive whereas the hero, in the traditional sense, is active and acts upon his opponents. Even though he may be in emo-tional and physical pain, his suffering is not that of the dark night journeyer, who has no choice but to undergo the or-deal. The spiritual journeyer is no hero, and spiritual adoles-cents seduced by romantic and faddish notions of the dark night would do well to read carefully and soberly John's writ-ings. The dark night is no momentary sally into suffering. It is an ordeal through which we stumble in anything but glori-ous fashion.

John also emphasizes suffering because it is the primary and usually the only manifestation of God's presence to us. As known mediators of God such as husband, children and lover are taken away through radical estrangement, there is necessarily experienced the pain of loss, not only loss of the emotional and physical presence of the loved one, but also the presence of God, who was mediated to us through that person. In our struggle to reclaim the loss, we meet the vital desire that enables us to act at all, and this desire is not without purpose, for though on the surface we may think our desire is to find the lost mediator, in fact it is to encounter that which was mediated — God. So our desire is our loving, and in our desiring/loving we meet God even though we do not yet understand at the level that exceeds intellectual understanding what is happening.[27] Our pain is our burden and our blessing; we cannot lay it down, only clasp it blindly, in an embrace that bears no resemblance whatsoever to that of the masochist who with his suffering picks it up and lays it down at will. We embrace our pain because we have to, not understanding why this desire that rises up as if out of nowhere impels us to continue.[28]

Let us touch upon the mystery of suffering with examples of women whose pain is not in direct relationship to the actions of other people, who may not receive our sympathy for being victims, as was the case of the woman whose husband was unfaithful. Imagine a Christian wife of many years' fidelity to her husband who unexpectedly finds herself in love outside of marriage. Whether that love is consummated physically or not is not the point because the devoted wife who has been loving God through her husband agonizes in the realization that she no longer is emotionally faithful to her husband and that he no longer is the central mediator of God in her life. Long accustomed to seeing herself as model wife whose role was to care for husband, children and home, she experiences in the failure to play this role a fall from perfection and in this failure and falling the illusion of knowing herself and the world shatters and she sees herself for what she is—mere creature.

In this situation the woman who has devotedly searched for God by emulating the model of mother and wife will try desperately to restore the model and revive the security of living in accord with it, but such return cannot be, and she will suffer unspeakable pain as the interior growth that is being realized through the fall is not yet realized by her. Counsel from church and friends will avail her little, for though she may endeavor to act resolutely on their advice, she vacillates and in vacillating blames herself even more and tries even more desperately to go back to the old ways.

Another example that demonstrates that emotions are no respecters of prudence and moral convention is the woman, let us say in marriage or convent, who comes to realize that she has homosexual tendencies too strong to be denied. Her response will be similar to the wife in love outside of marriage, and the pain of loss will be equally intense.

In countless situations today women are undergoing the loss of traditional values, systems and relationships to the distress of themselves and their loved ones and to the dismay of those in institutions affected by their experience. When the loss is radical, that is, when it affects our total being, is unplanned and unwanted, reduces us to emotional, intellectual and physical helplessness, leaves us suspended between a darkened past and a dark future so that all of our being rails against the loss, then we are undergoing our dark night. When we cry in anguish "God, my God," when we feel empty of all meaning, when we do not know who this God is to whom we dumbly cling, then we are undergoing our dark night. No hint of exotic adventure here, just groping and grasping.

Clearly I am not referring to women whose commitments are slight and fleeting, nor is the dark night John describes the experience of the spiritually lukewarm.[29] It comes to those who love intensely, but not yet freely, those who must be liberated from their selfish dependency on anything outside of themselves that mediates existence and fosters the illusion that they have mastery over themselves and the world. It is the experience of those who are faithful and devoted to values, concepts, structures and relationships but whose dependency on such commitments must be stripped away so that they can confront the fact of existence — dependency itself. In this confrontation with dependency itself, with our creatureliness, we meet God heart to heart. This is the experience of those who are being transformed in loving to loving, a transformation that because of the high cost of suffering is glimpsed but darkly at moments — moments of such intense beauty as to fire the desire that impels them forward. This is the experience of women who are made to relinquish dependency on husband, child and church, made to stand in the solitude of dark desire, a scandal to themselves and their society.

If *all* the principles which I have explained are in effect (not only one or two of them), and if we feel ourselves simply "hanging on," our prayer a groaning "Here I am, God, I love You" that tears through our being, there may occur the breakthrough that we cannot explain and cannot make happen. It is the transformation that gives birth to the loving person of whom John sings in his beautiful canticle:

> *If I'm not seen again*
> *in the old places, on the village ground,*
> *say of me: lost to men.*[30]

Thus are we, lost to men . . . found to God, found by God, found in God.

In our dark journey of unknowing we are taken through and beyond the symbols, structures, concepts and relationships on which we depended for knowledge about God and which we attempted to control as a conscious or unconscious endeavor to know and control the divine. This ordeal of being freed from dependency to dependency itself and from the illusion of control brings us into God, for as Meister Eckhart says, "When God finds a naughted soul whose self and whose activity have been brought to naught by means of grace, God works his eternal work in her above grace, raising her out of her created nature. Here," Eckhart continues, "God naughts himself in the soul, and then neither God nor soul is left."[31]

In God, oned with God, through God, a burn of love, with neither inside nor outside, the soul, to quote John in his *Living Flame of Love*, "has entered into consciousness of God,"[32] and all of her—body, mind, emotions, spirit—are God's. Loving God passionately and intimately, with no intermediary whatsoever, we know that God is closer to us than we are to ourselves. As Eckhart says, "God must be very I, I very God, so consummately one that this he and this I are one is, in this is-ness working one work eternally."[33] He exhorts us: "Love him as he is: a non-God, a non-spirit, a non-Person, a not-image; as sheer, pure, limpid unity, alien from all duality. And in this one let us sink down eternally from nothingness to nothingness" (p. 274).

For us women today who strive to live spiritually free and

unique, what does it mean to sink down from "nothingness to nothingness"? Are we to reject all formal relationships and surrender commitments? Must the loss of fidelity in marriage be the loss of marriage? The loss of belief in the Eucharist be the loss of faith itself? Must the loss of any value, concept, person or institution that has mediated the presence of God mean for us the loss of God? In the wisdom of apophatic mysticism the answer is an emphatic "No." For in the tradition of dark knowing God is the not-God who exceeds any form or idea we may have set up as God, and there is discovered to us that loss is gain, concealment is revelation, and darkness is light.

Through the dark night there comes the gain, the revelation, the knowing and the light such as neither we nor any human could imagine, conceive of or hope for. For that which is revealed is utterly new, greater than and other than the sum of all specific options and hopes that we or others could have composed as we were undergoing the ordeal.

The feminist mystic, then, is she who suffers through loss to taste the immeasurable delight of knowing herself as pure creature, loved uniquely and freed to love uniquely. It may be that unique loving exacts modifications in our lives that take the form of divorce, change of profession, or leaving a religious order, but the radical change that occurs within, transforming how we see and know ourselves and the world, this change does not make of events like divorce a uniform necessity. Indeed, if we ponder the lives of mystics in both Christianity and other religions, we observe that even though they had to make changes so that the externals of their living were consonant with the inner impulse, they did so from within established structures, to the benefit of the institution as well as themselves.

The fruit of the dark night is to find ourselves within reality, creating with and through it. Whereas we previously stood outside of concepts, images, structures and people and in so doing fostered the illusion that we controlled them, there is now no longer an outside or inside, a here or there, a this or that. The feminist mystic is within a within that is without a without.

If, for example, in the dark night our belief in a particular Christian symbol like the cross is destroyed, this does not mean that the reality of the cross has died to us. It is rather that dependence upon conceptual interpretation of the symbol dies, leaving disclosed the greater reality that the symbol was intended to express and which the mind could not grasp. Perhaps the night was a stripping away of dependency upon a husband, extinction of the belief that through him the fact and value of one's existence could be known and managed. In both of these cases the duality of subject and object is destroyed, baring reality itself and freeing us to see and know uniquely (not intellectually) the oneness that is all.

This seeing obtains in all aspects of living for the feminist mystic. She sees other people and institutions as well as symbols, values and ideas from within, in the reality that recognizes neither division nor separation, in the "pure limpid unity alien from all duality." The feminist mystic can remain within traditional relationships and structures because her seeing is unfragmented. In a process that acutely distressed herself and loved ones and strained if not severed all sorts of commitments, she has been freed from the inadequacy of interpretations and beliefs that theology and tradition attach to the outside of reality. She has been freed to a loving which itself is "alien from all duality," and in this loving she is freed to God—irrespective of the language she might employ to express and adore her Loving-God.

We do not ask from Christianity what it cannot give or what is not rightfully ours. It is our spiritual heritage we claim, *our* dark night, to be endured here and now. We must take back the night. How else are we to see the Light?

NOTES

1. Elaine Pagels, *The Gnostic Gospels* (New York: Random House, 1979).

2. *The Mystical Theology* in F.C. Happold's *Mysticism: A Study and an Anthology* (Penguin Books, 1963), p. 212.

3. *Meister Eckhart: A Modern Translation*, tr. Raymond B. Blakney (New York: Harper & Row, 1941), p. 102.

4. *The Cloud of Unknowing* in Happold's *Mysticism*, p. 308.

5. John Ruysbroeck, *The Adornment of the Spiritual Marriage* in Happold's *Mysticism*, p. 291.

6. All references to *Ascent of Mount Carmel* and *Dark Night of the Soul* are to the editions and translations by E. Allison Peers (Garden City, New York: Doubleday & Company, Inc., Image Books, 1958 and 1959 respectively).

7. *Ascent*, Book II, chapter 13.

8. *Dark Night*, Book I, chapter 9.

9. The classic statement on subject-object knowing in terms of how women have been objectified is Simone de Beauvoir's *The Second Sex* (New York: Alfred A. Knopf, Inc., 1952).

10. This dark and confused knowledge John calls general spiritual supernatural understanding. For treatment of it see the *Ascent*, Book II, chapters 24, 25, 26, 27 and 32. He says in chapter 24, for example, that "although these visions of spiritual substances cannot be unveiled and be clearly seen in this life by the understanding, they can nevertheless be felt in the substance of the soul, with the sweetest touches and unions, all of which belongs to spiritual feelings, whereof, with the Divine favour, we shall treat presently." He continues: "We shall speak of this when we treat of the dark and confused mystical understanding which remains to be described, wherein we shall show how, by means of this dark and loving knowledge, God is united with the soul in a lofty and Divine degree; for, after some manner, this dark and loving knowledge, which is faith, serves as a means to Divine union in this life, even as, in the next life, the light of

glory serves as an intermediary to the clear vision of God" (pp. 219-220). See all of the *Dark Night*, with particular attention to Book I, chapter 9 and Book II, chapters 3, 4, 5, 9, 16, 17 and 24.

11. John is especially to the point in the *Ascent*, Book III, chapters 35-44 when he treats the need to be detached from dependency on religious images, oratories and ceremonies.

12. *The Life of Teresa of Jesus*, ed. and tr. E. Allison Peers (Garden City, New York: Doubleday & Company, Inc., Image Books, 1960), p. 247.

13. St. Teresa of Avila, *The Interior Castle*, ed. and tr. E. Allison Peers (Garden City, New York: Doubleday & Company, Inc., Image Books, 1961), p. 210-211.

14. One of many occasions on which John gives warning in this area: "It now remains, then, to be pointed out that the soul must not allow its eyes to rest upon that outer husk—namely, figures and objects set before it supernaturally. These may be presented to the exterior senses, as are locutions and words audible to the ear; or, to the eyes, visions of saints, and of beauteous radiance; or perfumes to the sense of smell; or tastes and sweetnesses to the palate; or other delights to the touch, which are wont to proceed from the spirit, a thing that very commonly happens to spiritual persons. Or the soul may have to avert its eyes from visions of interior sense, such as imaginary visions, all of which it must renounce entirely. It must set its eyes only upon the spiritual good which they produce, striving to preserve it in its works and to practise that which is for the due service of God, paying no heed to those representations nor desiring any pleasure of sense. And in this way the soul takes from these things only that which God intends and wills—namely, the spirit of devotion—for there is no other important purpose for which He gives them; and it casts aside that which He would not give if these gifts could be received in the spirit without it, as we have said—namely, the exercise and apprehension of the senses." (*Ascent*, Book II, chapter 17, p. 167).

15. Karl Barth, "The Doctrine of Creation" in *Women and Religion*, ed. Elizabeth Clark and Herbert Richardson (New York: Harper & Row, 1977), p. 254.

16. For future reading consult the many references given by Clare B. Fischer in *Breaking Through: A Bibliography of Women and Religion* (Berkeley, California: The Graduate Theological Union Library, 1980).

17. From *The Poems of St. John of the Cross*, tr. John Frederick Nims (New York: Grove Press Inc., 1959).

18. John says in the *Dark Night*, Book II, chapter 5: "Beneath the power of this oppression and weight the soul feels itself so far from being favoured that it thinks, and correctly so, that even that wherein it was wont to find

some help has vanished with everything else, and that there is none who has pity upon it." Again: ". . . when this Divine contemplation assails the soul with a certain force, in order to strengthen it and subdue it, it suffers such pain in its weakness that it nearly swoons away. This is especially so at certain times when it is assailed with somewhat greater force; for sense and spirit, as if beneath some immense and dark load, are in such great pain and agony that the soul would find advantage and relief in death" (p. 103).

19. See the *Dark Night*, Book II, chapter 7: ". . . there is added to all this (because of the solitude and abandonment caused in it by this dark night) the fact that it finds no consolation or support in any instruction nor in a spiritual master" (p. 110).

20. John describes the pain in several moving passages, one of which is in *Dark Night*, Book II, chapter 6: "The Divine assails the soul in order to renew it and thus to make it Divine; and, stripping it of the habitual affections and attachments of the old man, to which it is very closely united, knit together and conformed, destroys and consumes its spiritual substance, and absorbs it in deep and profound darkness. As a result of this, the soul feels itself to be perishing and melting away, in the presence and sight of its miseries, in a cruel spiritual death, even as if it had been swallowed by a beast and felt itself being devoured in the darkness of its belly, suffering such anguish as was endured by Jonas in the belly of that beast of the sea. For in this sepulchre of dark death it must needs abide until the spiritual resurrection which it hopes for" (p. 104).

21. See all of chapter 23 in her autobiography.

22. John describes the loneliness of the dark night in *Dark Night*, Book II, chapter 6: "It feels, too, that all creatures have forsaken it, and that it is condemned by them, particularly by its friends" (p. 105).

23. See *Dark Night*, Book II, chapter 7: "The afflictions and constraints of the will are now very great likewise, and of such a kind that they sometimes transpierce the soul with a sudden remembrance of the evils in the midst of which it finds itself, and with the uncertainty of finding a remedy for them. And to this is added the remembrance of times of prosperity now past; for as a rule souls that enter this night have had many consolations from God, and have rendered Him many services, and it causes them the greater grief to see that they are far removed from that happiness, and unable to enter into it" (p. 108).

24. From chapter 20 in her autobiography: ". . . but I think it is true of the soul when no comfort comes to it from Heaven, and it is not in Heaven, and when it desires no earthly comfort, and is not on earth either, but is, as it were, crucified between Heaven and earth; and it suffers greatly, for no help comes to it either from the one hand or from the other" (p. 194).

25. For the purgation of memory, understanding and will as the sources of specific hope, belief and desire, see *Dark Night*, Book II, chapter 16.

26. For further descriptions and explanations of pain, see *Dark Night*, Book II, chapters 5, 6, 7, 8.

27. See Teresa's classic statement in her autobiography: "The will must be fully occupied in loving, but it cannot understand how it loves; the understanding, if it understands, does not understand how it understands, or at least can comprehend nothing of what it understands. It does not seem to me to be understanding, because, as I say, it does not understand itself. Nor can I myself understand this" (p. 180).

28. There is brief respite, which I have indicated by the awareness of desire. See John, *Dark Night*, Book II, chapter 7: " Thus, being exhausted, withered and thoroughly tried in the fire of this dark contemplation, and having driven away every kind of evil spirit (as with the heart of the fish which Tobias set on the coals), it may have a simple and pure disposition, and its palate may be purged and healthy, so that it may feel the rare and sublime touches of Divine love, wherein it will see itself divinely transformed, and all the contrarieties, whether actual or habitual, which it had aforetime, will be expelled, as we are saying" (p. 122).

29. See John, *Dark Night*, Book I, chapter 9: "There is thus a great difference between aridity and lukewarmness, for lukewarmness consists in great weakness and remissness in the will and in the spirit, without solicitude as to serving God; whereas purgative aridity is ordinarily accompanied by solicitude, with care and grief as I say, because the soul is not serving God" (pp. 64-65).

30. Nims, "The Spiritual Canticle," p. 9.

31. Happold's *Mysticism*, pp. 272-273.

32. St. John of the Cross, *Living Flame of Love*, ed. and tr. E. Allison Peers (Garden City, New York: Doubleday & Company, Inc., Image Books, 1962), p. 53.

33. Happold's *Mysticism*, p. 274.

CHAPTER 3

Immanent Mother

🍎 *Meinrad Craighead*

The creative spirit I know within me has the face and the force of a woman. She is my Mother, my Mothergod, my generatrix, the divine immanence I experience signified in all of creation. I first experienced Her when I was still a youngster, about seven years old.

I think everything and everyone slept that hot summer afternoon in Little Rock. I sat with my dog in a cool place on the north side of my grandparents' clapboard home. Hydrangeas flourished there, shaded from the heat. The domed blue flowers were higher than our heads. I held the dog's head, stroking her into sleep. But she held my gaze. As I looked into her eyes I realized that I would never travel further than into this animal's eyes. They were as deep, as bewildering, as unattainable as a night sky. Just as mysterious was a clear awareness of water within me, the sound in my ears, yet resounding from my breast. I gazed into the dog's eyes and listened to the sound of rushing water inside me. I understood "This is who God is. My Mother is water and she is inside me and I am in the water." This intuition was to be an irrevocable orientation to the primordial Matrix, a lifetime preoccupation with and persistence toward the source.

I spent the rest of the afternoon digging a hole. I spaded and shoveled the hole for many days thereafter, until the walls of the cavity collapsed, my act of worship exhausted.

Soon after this, in a Chicago Catholic elementary school, I came upon a photograph in a textbook and I recognized my Mothergod. It was a picture of the Venus of Willendorf. The recognition was immediate and certain. I knew this was she whom I had heard in the water and whose face I sought beyond the water and beyond the dog's eyes. This discovery brought a sense of relief and well-being and gratitude that has never diminished.

But she had no face. The Venus was crowned with waves of water, covering the head, overshadowing the face. It was her entire body that spoke, her breast-belly body, a thick bulb rooted, pushing up a halo of water, the water that moved within me. Thereafter it was she whom I sought to see always, and being with her was undoubtedly the origin of my desire for a life of contemplative prayer and to be an artist. I had then, and still have, but one essential prayer: "Show me your face."

Through half a lifetime of Christian worship my secret worship of God the Mother has been the sure ground of my spirituality. The participation in her body, in the natural symbols and rhythms of all organic life and the actualization of her symbols in my life as an artist, have been a steadfast protection against the negative patriarchal values of Christianity, the faith I still profess. Like many other women who choose to reinvest their Christian heritage rather than abandon it, my spirituality is sustained by a commitment to a personal vision that affirms woman as an authentic image of the Divine and enlightens, informs and enriches the orthodox image of the transcendent Father God.

Out of the anxiety, the lack of meaning and sense of disin-
tegration that women suffer in a totally masculine church, we
must make meaning for ourselves on our own terms, ex-
ploring the history of women's unique spiritual experience
and discovering a vision to which we can be personally committed. It is a quest for each individual woman and it takes us
back to a time when God was worshipped as Mother.

Each of the many stories of the female Deity (and there are
thousands of these myths) is but one portion of a vast tapestry
that, seen as a whole, forms a collective description of a feminine attitude toward life, death, after-death and our place
in the universe. It is when contemporary women are willing
to share their private intuitions, take up the thread of their
personal mythologies and tell their own stories that this tapestry will be continued and a collective experience made visible
today.

The original pattern of creation still in-forms all of creation. Everything that is is rooted in something that was and is
passing on to something that will be. Mythology makes this
continuum visible. Myths, the ancient legends and symbolic
tales of the human race, live eternally in our religions, litera-
tures and arts. They live when and because they are individ-
ually internalized; we re-new them. And we are renewed by
them. Through the myths our basic psychic needs — our deepest fears and sorrows, our joys and aspirations, our drives and
desires — are evoked, confronted and directed. They awaken
and maintain a sense of awe and gratitude in relationship to
the mystery of the universe and our human existence within
it. In symbolic, metaphoric language they tell us the nature
of the universe, where we belong in it with others and how to
discover our deepest identity, our organic sense of being with
the rest of life. Their accurate insights into human aims and

ends amaze us. The questions they raise still vex us. Basically they ask: What relationships can exist between a changing world of finite forms and their eternal Infinite source, between the manifest and the unmanifest, between multivalent reality and an incomprehensible unity? These questions are most poetically and ingeniously articulated in many of the creation myths, where practical human creative imagining reflects, mimics and describes the Divine activity in all of creation. Myths are preoccupied with that impossible point of contact between the finite and the Infinite, that unrest that moves the depth of our being, urging us into spiritual quest. It is inspired restlessness that drives a person to an end that is vaster than the completion of self, the unrest that marks the fundamental direction of the heart toward something transcendent.

At the source of our deepest self is a mysterious unknown ever eluding our grasp. We can never possess it except as that mystery which keeps at a distance. The heart's quest is toward this unknown. There is no respite in the task of getting beyond the point we have already reached because the Spirit stands further on. She stands at the end of every road we may wish to travel by. The entire movement of our being seems to focus on this single point of identity, which will be realized in the encounter. We never "catch up with" who we fundamentally are.

Life may be understood as an uninterrupted duration, our existence completely open to our past. Everything we have experienced is carried into the present and pushes at consciousness. But we are generally successful in blocking off our own past, concerned not with it, or the present moment, but concentrating rather on future engagements.

When we face the present moment we seem unable to hold

it, be within it, live it fully. The stream of existence flows urgently toward the future and we lose the moments that measure and make our lives. Some people do seem able to, or will themselves to, live in the present moment, understanding its capacity, which holds the whole of life in one undivided present. But most people tend to feel the past as remote, no longer there, unreal "mythological fantasy." The practical, pragmatic person concentrates on the future, grasping from the past only what will enlighten or be useful for future experience. Seemingly with years at our disposal we plan, compete, achieve, acquire, progress at an ever quickening pace, seeking power, longing for future fulfillment.

The experience of the undivided present, life as uninterrupted duration, rests within the female principle as the elemental and unifying force. The characteristically meditative spirit of the female and its initial, powerful impress on our earliest human societies suggests a reason for its gradual demise and eventual submersion in patriarchal cultures. The reason may be inherent in the existential inability of most people, women and men alike, to be fully open to this essential reality—that we only have life from moment to moment. The pace of active future-dwellers, caught up in the progression of linear time, necessarily overtakes and governs those who do not live in future-time but desire only the fullest content of each moment.

Leonardo da Vinci has said:

> Everything, everyone, wants to go back to the original chaos, like the butterfly that insists on being burned in the candle flame. Man is always longing for next spring, next summer, future months, new years. It always seems to him that the thing he lusts after never comes soon enough. Yet he never realizes that all he is asking

> for, in fact, is his own destruction, his own unmaking.
> And this desire, so unconscious and deep within him, is
> of his very essence. He has the spirit in him and this
> spirit, being aware that it is shut up in a human body, is
> always longing to get back to the one who put it there.

For fourteen years I lived out the Christian life within a monastic context. My gradual disillusionment with monastic life and my unease grew in proportion to my realization of my sisters' narrow and rigid expectations of what that life should be. The community mind sought the survival of a social and spiritual tradition. I thought monastic life was about freedom of spirit and the risks of an unorthodox life. For most of the nuns, the enclosed life ensured a continuation of the inherited security of English homes and institutions, which had conditioned them to play expected roles. The monastery offered no possibility of escaping this conditioning; indeed, the life continually reinforced it. Although I desired to live a monastic life, I could not do so among dependent, inauthentic people estranged from themselves. I often had the feeling of living among ghosts absorbed in playing roles in one repetitive script, acting in order to receive acceptance and approval. For women with little imagination and experiential resources the inherited communal image was their only identity and "rule of life." Increasingly my own spiritual orientation and creative work became so opposed to the communal heteronomy and the worship of an exalted masculine god-image that it was necessary for me to leave.

While I continue to believe in the Christian mysteries, this decision signified a personal reevaluation of patriarchal Christianity. It was impossible, disintegrating, to support a liturgy that legitimized and worshipped an exclusively male God and encouraged women to live limited, subordinated, clerically defined lives. When the gap between liturgy and life becomes intolerable, when meaningful rituals are denied women, we are driven to seek alternatives that may really formulate our deeply personal spiritual energies and express our inmost prayer.

We may remain engaged on the conscious level with the many problems besetting a dispirited church, but if we are to survive, to hold together the levels of meaning in our lives, then private spontaneity is indispensable for spiritual growth. Religions obsessed with security, rectitude, dogmatic definitions and codes of perfection show an intolerance of the ambiguities that pervade human existence. Certitude weakens the imagination and does not strengthen faith. We must be willing to risk encounters at the edgelessness of all reality, to face the anxiety of uncertain and ambiguous reality. Only the abiding faith in the wisdom of the Spirit can encourage us in this, can hearten us to resist conformity and complacency.

We know that ultimate spiritual Reality is neither male nor female, nor both. Yet, all religious language in the ancient myths of all peoples and in the scriptures of the great religions uses this basic sexual metaphor, following human clues for investigating divine reality and activity. Thus, the qualities of human character and experience and all the paradoxes of human nature are transferred to the divine, as we seek to love or assuage a transcendent and immanent divine power. Yet, finally, "like-unto" cannot be definitive, and the metaphors necessarily express a limited, fractured and diverse image of the incomprehensible fullness and bewildering otherness of Divine Reality. We must fall back on "God has many faces and many names," and it cannot be otherwise. Here we remain, locked in linguistic limitations, our human languages too finite to name the Infinite.

The use of exclusively male language in Christian worship continually reiterates the limited revelation of God as a male being and prevents women from valuing and expressing themselves and their very different spiritual experience. Male-dominated Christian teaching and practice, instead of affirming the Female as an authentic image of God and encouraging women's mature autonomy, has significantly distorted the biblical revelation (" . . . in the divine image God created them; male and female God created them") and alienated women from their deepest and truest understanding of God as Mother.

A woman's spiritual quest in God the Mother awakens her to forces of energy within herself, yet larger than self, transcending self, deeply connecting her with the cyclic movements of creation and personally with her foremothers whose energies still surge through her body, her Tree of Life. The tree and moon are two of many female symbols in the world of ordinary, daily sensory experience by which the Mother Spirit is manifest in the goodness of creation. When we pray through our bodies we energize our will to transform and be transformed within our rhythmic changes and seasons. To do so is to acknowledge and affirm our nature explicitly and to glorify God the Mother by our very womanhood.

Spirituality must encompass every dimension of human life. A responsible spirituality must be the expression of the whole woman. Women have been withheld from full participation in the Christian mysteries for so long that to remain Christian one is driven to operate intuitively, trusting the inner Spirit to awaken, encourage and direct. When the religious impulse is frustrated in external liturgical expression, it is channeled within, running more deeply and directly in one's deepest being, nourishing new insights and levels of understanding.

A woman sheds blood from her body and from her spirit. Memories stir and incubate; they are remembered, reformed and animated into imagery. Whether we are weaving tissue in the womb or weaving imagery in the soul, our work is sexual: the work of conception, gestation and birth. Our spirituality should center on the affirmation of our female sexuality in its seasons of cyclic change. Our feminine existence is connected to the metamorphoses of nature: the pure potential of water, the transformative power of blood, the seasonal rhythms of the earth, the cycles of lunar dark and light. Within nature we too transform matter, giving form to elemental energy, handling water and fire, cooking and baking, bearing and healing, tending and gathering, making from the earth's materials.

Whether or not a woman actually conceives, she always carries the essence of the germinative ocean within her, the flux of the energy in formless potential. It is a spiritual fertility, full from within, a woman's inheritance, not dependent on external catalyst. So, too, the artist is always pregnant from within, a container of endless potential transformations, abandoned to the fertilizing powers of the imagination, actualizing unknown faces parthenogenetically.

In solitude our deepest intuitions of an indwelling personal God Spirit are confirmed, the Mothergod who never withdraws from us and whose presence is our existence and the life of all that is. Her unveiled glory is too great for us to behold; she hides her face. But we find her face in reflection, in sacred guises, mediated through the natural, elemental symbols. It is the response to them that matters, the desire to receive with animation those messages carried through our nervous senses and the will to focus their energy and transform it into worship.

The purest acts of worship acknowledging her presence within us are the simple, significant gestures toward the natural objects outside us — touching a stone or a tree, drinking water and milk, being with fire or standing in the wind or listening to birds. Seeing the parts, realizing the whole, connecting inner and outer. The worship is the sensible focus, the will to be still, to receive, to be with the bird or the grass, addressing its otherness, confessing her utterly divine otherness in the perfection of every living creature.

The simplest actions should be done with a full realization of their significance, giving them an opportunity to communicate their elemental meaning in our lives — pouring water from a jug, kneading bread, breaking an egg, observing the unconscious movements of those we love, working the earth, paring vegetables, singing a song. Ordinary, daily life is weighted with mystery and beauty. To a meditative spirit, the smallest observation or activity can startle the imagination to wakefulness and a sense of wonder at the significance of being. They speak plainly. And apart from the multifarious marvels of natural creation there is sufficient poetry in any well-made article of human craftsmanship to engage our attention for a lifetime. Or in the innocent presentations of human traditions — a handful of grain, a basket of blackberries, a vase of flowers, a clutch of hen's eggs, a board of cheese, a family photograph, a table laid for a meal.

These are the symbols for a woman's spirituality and their importance cannot be overestimated. The experience of grace, gratuitous divine life imparted to us, cannot be recognized or understood without the help of natural symbols derived from our ordinary sensory experiences. They point the way to the sacred incarnate in our midst. They are the simple things all round us, perceived on the plane of immediate experience, but simultaneously expressing infinite mystery. Any natural object can represent the sacred, declare its presence and move us to worship the vibrating undercurrent of divine energy. Each is but a fragment of the "world" body (as each of us is), yet through it we may apprehend the incarnate presence of the holy in all of creation. Through them God our Mother communicates with us through her body, within her own mysterious creation.

We are all consecrated by the gift of life; bonded in that unutterable sense of wonder in the chance for existence. We stand before the incomprehensible, mirroring for life's moment all the mysteries of energy and transformed matter, grateful for having seen the rounded form of earth silhouetted against infinity, sunlight in a field of wheat, moonlight in an apple orchard, rain and running water, fire and the face of a child.

We know instinctively that these sacred moments, in our "secret garden," are intensely private, unto ourselves; that articulation would dissipate the communication. These are the silent ideo-rhythmic responses, our fleeting moments of understanding the interrelatedness of the spiritual and the material. We should enter our gardens in a spirit of gratitude. But these intuitions can also inform the traditional Christian sacramental liturgies and deepen our communal participation in these ancient rites. When our bodies are liturgically anointed with holy oil and immersed in water, when the fragrance of incense is in our nostrils, salt and honey on our tongue, and the light of the Easter candle in our eyes, we are physically signed with the earth symbols of the divine Generatrix. These are rituals of interpenetration, the mingling of human and terrestrial with Divine Being. "I in thee and thou in me."

When we eat the food of Thanksgiving, the Eucharist, we participate in the Mother's incarnate substance: the bread her body, the blood her milk, sacramentally transformed into the body and blood of Christ. When Jesus says, "This is my body; This is my blood," he acknowledges his human participation in two of the most profound elemental symbols: grain and fruit. And he actualizes these symbols in the universal liturgy of remembering: a meal.

"We celebrate the memory of . . . " is an oft repeated phrase in the Christian liturgy and is a good reminder of the common alliance of all worship throughout the ages. All religions celebrate remembering: memories of theophanies and numinous cosmic manifestations, memories of divine visitations and holy ancestors. To remember, and to celebrate the memory, is to safeguard the happening from generation to generation. Herein lies the root coherence of art and religion. Both make out of remembering: religion through ritual, art through the imagery that slips spontaneously from the unconscious recesses of personal memories.

The artist's function is to animate what we remember, what the senses have let in, what the imagination has sorted and stored. Like a woman's form and function, the artist is a cavity of ripening imagery, admitting everything to the bed and transforming it, allowing multiple faces to evolve and break from the containing vessel, an unbroken story of emergence.

How much of the inner and outer world have we seen through our mother's eyes before we see with our own? What soul energies absorbed and memories transmitted, what relationships inherited, what immeasurable layers of her psychic life are pressed into our embryonic fabric while we float in the amniotic womb waters?

We are born remembering; we are born connected. The thread of personal myth winds through the matriarchal labyrinth, from womb to womb, to the faceless source, which is the place of origination. Every drawing I make begins from this deep inner source where live my mother and her mother and all my foremothers, the memories of the childhood places and experiences which they still inhabit. What gestates in this personal underworld waits for passage from one stage of life to another, memories waiting for transformation into imagery. I draw from my own myth of personal origin and each picture is a realization of this story and is connected to the ancient image of the Godmother in art and mythology. Every drawing is a quest for origin, a return to the source following the hidden threads in the labyrinthine matrix. Making is worship.

All creative work may be considered a re-formation of exemplary mythological thought. Anyone involved in creating anything new ritually reenacts, consciously or unconsciously, basic primordial concepts, all of which are fundamental expressions of the female cosmic force. And each person's life is in creative evolution, moving on to what will be from what has been. Just to be in the world is to be in the continuous process of becoming, to be caught up in the dynamics of creation, constituting the world by being and doing and making. Stasis, induced by fear and timidity, is death, personal and communal.

The Mother has but one law: "Create; make as I do make." Obedience to this law is the deepest obedience and the worthiest worship of her. Make, transform one substance into another, press form into chaos, mold material into spiritual reality, fashion potential into actual, change one form of energy into another. Transmute blood into milk, clay into vessel, feeling into movement, wind into song, egg into child, fiber into cloth, stone into crystal, memory into image, body into worship.

CHAPTER 4

The Courage To Be Alone—
In and Out of Marriage
🍎 *Margaret R. Miles*

The topic of aloneness is one I've thought about for quite a few years—whether I wanted to or not! It's a difficult topic to write about because, on the one hand, it's an intimate topic; on the other hand, it's an enormous topic, requiring a historic and cosmic perspective. The variety of approaches to the topic of aloneness are reflected in the many scholarly and popular books that analyze different aspects of aloneness. One could deal with the topic of aloneness by distilling the best insights of these books, or one could speak personally, describing what I find useful, formulating the ideas and images that work for me. I have chosen the latter approach, although the academic and the personal approaches are not entirely distinct, and there will be a weaving together of things I've learned from the historic Christian authors I study and things I'm learning from living.

These ideas are personal, perhaps even more clearly personal than all ideas are personal, and as a historian, I'm aware of our constant temptation to isolate ideas from the lives that pressed people to the ideas, and then support and reinforce the ideas. So I want to take a moment to underline and insist on the connection of the ideas I'll be presenting with my life, which, in painful and joyful seasons, brought me to these ideas. I will give you a bit of statistical auto- biography in order to help you imagine the life out of which I speak: I have been married twice, once for twelve years and once for seven years, and I've been divorced twice. I have two no-longer children, a son, twenty-two, and a daughter, twenty-four. I began college when my children began school, and I continued almost nonstop for the next thirteen years, never imagining that I would one day com- plete a doctorate. I continued quarter by quarter because it still—and increasingly—felt abundantly worth doing, be- cause learning is addictive, and because I couldn't distin- guish between academic learning and the process of learn- ing things about myself. One of the factors that started this process was, when I was twenty-two, a punctured ulcer, fol- lowed by seven years of psychotherapy. You wouldn't imme- diately think that going to school would be just the very thing for a person with a minister husband, two small chil- dren, and an ulcer. It probably isn't what you'd prescribe! But for me, it was good; the ulcer gradually and totally vanished.

I will not begin by defining "aloneness" because the whole essay will attempt to clarify ideas of what aloneness is and to ask if there is an aloneness that we can affirm and enjoy, not just as a respite from the pressure of others, but on a contin- uing basis as the ground of all our relationships. Rather, I'll begin by suggesting that the states we call "aloneness" and those in which we are in intimate daily relationship with an- other—or other—human beings are not the absolutely oppo- site conditions that we have thought them, but that there is, in living alone, a surprisingly strong ingredient of introjected relationships. For reasons I will try to show, I cannot speak of aloneness without speaking of relationship.

That voice that speaks to us constantly from inside about how we're doing and whether we're OK—whose is it? Is it the voice of our father when we were four, annoyed and anxious that we won't "turn out" well? Is it the voice of our mother, perhaps, indulgently sympathetic, but without critical evaluation of our situation and helpful, or even playful, suggestions of other possibilities? Is it the voice of an adult friend laughing at us, but in a gentle, affirming way, thoughtfully evaluative of our situation? When one lives alone, the voices that had directed everything from the wings now come right out on stage.

And there is, in relationship with others, both the need to recognize the irreducible aloneness of human beings who have to do all the very most important human tasks alone: being born, learning, dying, and the frequent realization that just in the most tender and fragile places of the psyche, we are often painfully alone. My image of this realization is a scene in the movie version of Arthur Miller's play *The Misfits*. In this scene Marilyn Monroe is walking up the long steps of a courthouse in Nevada where she has established the necessary residence to get a divorce. Suddenly her estranged husband appears; he has flown there to try to stop the proceedings. He begs her to return to him, but she refuses and looking at him says, "If I'm going to be alone, I want to be by myself."

One treatment for the terror of aloneness in relationship has been proposed by Shelden Vanauken in the recent book *A Severe Mercy*. Describing his early relationship with his wife, he writes:

> ... the killer of love is creeping separateness. Taking
> love for granted.... Ceasing to do things together.
> Finding separate interests. We raised the Shining Barri-
> er against creeping separateness.... We rejected sepa-
> rate activities whether bridge or shooting or sailing,
> because they would lead to creeping separateness; on the
> other hand, if one of us liked anything, the other, in the
> name of sharing must learn to like it too ... each of us
> must read every book the other had read, even children's
> books.... We went to plays and concerts together and if
> one couldn't go the other didn't.... [1]

This book describes one of the most herculean efforts I
have ever seen to eliminate aloneness. The three reviews I
read were effusive in their praise, attesting the massive
human longing not to have to experience aloneness. But if
this solution is impossible or unattractive, and the realization
comes to us that we are, even in the midst of relationships,
alone, cutting through our defenses against seeing this, the
intricately worked defenses and illusions of indispensability
and importance, it is painful, but a place to begin. For me
this realization came when a dear friend, thirty years old
when I was twenty-six, woke up one morning when her four-
month-old baby cried; she had thirty seconds of convulsions
and died. Her sudden death was shocking and painful to me;
but when her husband married again in three months,
awareness of my own aloneness surfaced in me. If a person
totally invested in the relationships that defined her for
herself could be this replaceable, I wondered about the
wisdom of the investment of my total self-esteem, energy,
and time in my husband and children. There was, in the terror I felt then, a terror deeper than the fear of death because
it was also fear of life.

But I didn't only feel the terror of aloneness in living and dying; I also felt a zest to understand and enjoy some things. I began to go to school, to paint, to play music. The realization and acceptance of aloneness came with a great deal of energy attached to it; I stopped doing things that made me feel dead, like watching TV and reading newspapers. It was a start.

I ask myself now why realizing my aloneness even when I wasn't "by myself" was such a shattering and reordering experience. To begin to answer this, we need to distinguish two feelings of aloneness, both of which I was experiencing: feelings of aloneness in the universe — or existential aloneness — and feelings of aloneness either within primary daily relationships or in the absence of these. I think you are probably more interested in hearing about the latter, but I will need to talk a bit about existential aloneness in order to get at the pressure on daily aloneness and relationship in our time.

First, the conceptual structuring of the world in which we live, the ideas that we have about the nature and meaning of the universe, are ideas we have inherited. These ideas form and educate the consciousness of each of us to select as significant experiences that emphasize our separateness as individuals, our isolation from each other and from the natural world; we live in a universe of consciousness in which we are trained to notice distances, gulfs to be bridged, gaps between human beings, between Creator and creature, and between souls and bodies. If you don't agree with this, I recommend to you Ernest Becker's *The Denial of Death* as a recent best-selling account of exactly this experience of disjunction, which he calls "*the* human experience." Having had these gaps emphasized for us for centuries, we predictably experience them, and then begin to talk very rapidly about relationship.

Now it's very curious that talk about relationship always

needs to begin by establishing the otherness of two entities: Nothing relates except by establishing itself as other than that to which it relates. For the first people who began to describe this new understanding of the world, who point out things that people have not selected for notice before, this must be done crudely with exaggerated statements about the otherness of the two entities; nobody immediately recognizes the distinctness. One example is the severe statements about the grossness of the body and the consummate beauty and dignity of the human soul in the late classical period; Aristotle had raised a problem which, once raised, no one could ignore—the relationship of soul and body. In order to describe relationship, philosophers had to describe separate entities that needed relating.

We have now become so accustomed to assuming that this is the necessary world view that we seldom realize the extent to which it generates—as well as attempts to deal with—the problem of aloneness-as-separateness. And if, in our time, we continue to assume the problems—the gaps—without accepting the solutions, the overcoming of these gaps as proposed by the people, many centuries ago, who formulated this world view, we find ourselves in difficulty. The world view that we irreversibly inhabit is one of disjunction, incongruity, and harshly felt contradictoriness, which then our description of relationship attempts to overcome. This world view, minused, as I will later show, of an important part of the overcoming of it, is largely responsible for our painful experience of existential aloneness.

Secondly, there is another reason why we feel terror at the realization of our aloneness. For the first reason, we used a wide-angle lens; a problem so large requires this kind of perspective; it can't be treated just locally and today. The second reason is also difficult to grasp, not because it lies so hugely over space and time, but because it lies so close to the bone, so at the base of our consciousness. This reason requires a microscope rather than a wide-angle lens: It lies in our individual beginnings. The original human experience of pleasure—the infant suckling—is at the same time relational and the first experience of the self in the world. And it is not immediately discriminated as to an experiencing self and a relationship with another human being. Yet, as the first experience, it becomes the unconscious model, the paradigm of pleasurable experience with which we move through life, longing to replicate the intense pleasure of this experience, a pleasure which is at the same time the first experience of one's own person and the first experience of relationship. The implications of this undifferentiated but normative experience of personal identity and relationship are of enormous importance; since these originate together, we feel that when relationship with someone of primary significance is threatened, our selfhood is also threatened.

In addition, our attention has almost always been drawn to the relational aspect of this strongly concentrated pleasure. The studies, for example, of the infant situation focus on the bonding aspect, and the importance of the infant remaining with the mother for the first half hour of life so that this bonding can occur. We have all heard the results of studies done after the Second World War on orphaned babies: the babies who were held, cuddled, played with and talked to grew and thrived, while most of the babies fed and cared for in every way, but without personal attention, died. This frightens us deeply, even as adults. We feel our dependency on the loving attention of others. Our attention remains on the relational aspect of every intensely pleasurable experience.

E. O. Wilson, for example, in the recent controversial book, *On Human Nature*, describes the primary function of sex as neither reproductive, nor the giving and receiving of pleasure. Not reproductive, he says, because human sex is one of the least efficient and effective methods of reproduction of any evolved species; and not giving and receiving of pleasure, because this could be accomplished without the heavy invesment of time and energy that we usually make in courtship; "Sex," he writes, "is in every sense a gratuitously consuming and risky activity."[2] Biologically, sexual reproduction is necessary for diversity and therefore adaptability; sociologically, "sexual practices are to be regarded first as bonding devices." In other words, from a sociobiological point of view, sex is the intensely pleasurable experience in which bonding occurs, a bonding potentially strong enough to sustain the tremendously difficult work of relationship.

Yes, but a person can also learn things of the first importance about her/himself in the highly concentrated consciousness of sex. This aspect of pleasure has been mined by the "consciousness-raising" groups. Their insistence on the importance of a constant awareness of the primacy of one's own aggrandizement in relationships makes the other person an object for one's own pleasure and enhancement. Consistently refusing to identify this pleasure and enhancement as the gift of the other, one feels oneself totally uncommitted, and sustains the relationship only while it's mutually serviceable. I attended a wedding several years ago that articulated this view of relationship perfectly. The traditional vows were taken: "in sickness and in health, for richer or for poorer . . . for as long as the relationship shall last." This may have been prescience; the relationship lasted another eight months!

Certainly one would learn a great deal about separateness in a series of such relationships. Perhaps it is necessary that some people in our culture explore these painful commitments to separateness as a corrective for the total investment of self, of longings, of enjoyment in a relationship that most of us who are in our forties or older received as a model as we grew up. In this model each person's aloneness was not recognized, much less treasured. Just in case you do not immediately recognize this model of relationship, let me give you a historical example and an image.

A brilliant and highly educated young woman wrote to her husband, in the early twelfth century; "My heart was not in me, but in you, and now, even more, if it is not with you, it is nowhere; truly, without you it cannot exist. At every stage of my life up to now, as God knows, I have feared to offend you rather than God, and tried to please you more than him." Rhetoric? I think it is, to some degree. Heloise and Abelard had ten years earlier retired to convent and monastery. It is an historian's problem to reformulate what these words might have meant in the context in which Heloise spoke them. But I think they very accurately describe and define, if we carry them to an intimate level of the psyche, a dominant American ideal of marriage, in the world in which most of us grew up.

"I have feared to offend you rather than God, and tried to please you more than him." Wouldn't this be accurate? Were we ever — as women — encouraged to conceive our lives as primarily constituted by being "in the image and likeness of God," with all that might imply about the actualization of this image, the intellectual work, the social responsibility, the self-knowledge and possible sacrifice — but not to another human being who stands in the same humanness and respon-

sibility? No, I think we were emphatically encouraged to exercise our whole potential for being and service on other human beings, usually husband and children. And we required
of them, then, that they meet our expectations, that they
keep us nourished with pleasant and reassuring self-images.
We attempted — but ever so subtly — to derive our being from
them.

The image I have of this model of relationship takes us a
step further in describing this unexamined and illegitimate
burden of demand placed on the other. It is a scene from Ing-
mar Bergman's *Cries and Whispers*. A young woman who
was living in her family home with her two sisters has become
fatally ill. After weakening painfully and gradually, she finally dies one afternoon. The minister is called, and last rites
are said. That evening, one of her sisters comes into the bed-
room to look at her and, gazing at her face, is startled to see a
tear coming from her closed eyes. The young woman has revived briefly, and as her sister bends over her, she seizes her
with a stranglehold, clutching her, begging her to stay with
her. Terrified, her sister struggles free and runs from the
room.

While this image may be overly dramatic in its condensa-
tion into one scene, it is a very useful image of what many of
us do, or have done, in less dramatic ways over a long period
of time. Perhaps we need also to correct the onesidedness of
the image of the "dead" woman attempting to appropriate
the life of the living woman; what we need, perhaps, is an image of mutual parasitism. Yet the image is valuable in dra-
matizing the fact that we can't appropriate life by taking it
from another human being. We can "take" their lives, but
this simply leaves both of us without. It's precisely because of
not being able to acknowledge our aloneness that we come, in

desperation, or mindlessly, through our conditioning, to annex the life of other human beings. I don't think women are really any more guilty than men; women are just becoming more conscious of our style of doing this, and confessing it more.

But there are reasons why we can't acknowledge our aloneness: we have not been able to see the shape of our aloneness, exactly what it means, where it lies, in a way that we could affirm because, I have said, our earliest experiences, and our strongest experiences, are composed of undifferentiated aspects of aloneness and of relationship. We perhaps never are taught, or learn, to discriminate within this field what is our own strength, our own pleasure, our own ability to be aware and to respond, and what is the other's generosity and goodness. We tend either to claim everything for ourselves and discount the other, or to attribute all the beauty, pleasure, and enjoyment of the relationship to the other. Also, I spoke of our world view that tends to describe separated entities in relationship. Yet this world view was itself a corrective of competing world views that perhaps erred in the direction of not sufficiently describing the possibility of individuality, of uniqueness, of responsibility. The important point is that there are other ways to think of human experience than as persons in relationship. There is no need, for example, to talk about relationship in the world view described by Plotinus—and he doesn't! "When we find no stop at which to declare a limit to our being, no place at which to say, 'Up to here, and no further, it is I,' we cease to rule ourselves out from the total of reality...."[3] This describes an undifferentiated self, which has infinite potential for identifying—for merging—with any grade of being, from the physical, with its notorious and painful instability, its tendency to sickness, old age, and death, to assimilation into the One. Self, then, is constituted by the order of being to which it turns and with which it consciously identifies.

In the Christian tradition we do not find the same picture of an undifferentiated self formed by its choice of a dwelling place. But there are ways of describing the *connections* of the self, which are largely ignored when we put all our attention and emphasis on the relationship of separate entities. The model of the connected self is, I think, an alternative or correction within our tradition for the isolated separateness of "selves" that our relationship model assumes. The Eastern Orthodox Church, for example, has emphasized the language and imagery of deification, or participation in the activity of God, which the author of the epistle of John indicated when he wrote, "God *is* love . . . no one has *seen* God at any time; if we love one another God dwells in us and his love is perfected in us" (1 John 4:12). We participate in the activity of God when we love; his activity and our activity are connected, inseparable. Also, Paul's use of the metaphor of the body to define the connectedness of human beings who form the Church is a very explicit and dramatic way to insist on a mutual participation that cannot be described with a separate-entities-in-relationship model. Within this conceptual framework, it makes no sense to speak of absolute aloneness.

But the dominant Christian world view emphasizes relationship. I think our situation of not being able to do with, and not being able to do without, relationship is largely the result of retaining this Christian-Western emphasis, while eliminating from our conceptual and emotional world any relationships except those with other human beings. At least on the cultural level in which we all participate and from which we receive our problems, we reject the historic Christian ordering of relationship in which the weights fall in places that can bear those weights. The weight, in our time, falls almost entirely on one point: primary daily intimate relationships, a point that has not been able to bear the weight, with most painful and wasteful results for human lives and energy. Even the wider relationships that had somewhat distributed the weight a generation or two ago — the relationship to one's nation, to groups and organizations, to relatives, to a profession — have collapsed as points that could bear the weight of the individual's primary longing and commitment. The whole weight has collapsed onto personal relationship.

Theology used to formulate ways of distributing the weight. Let me give an example. Augustine expressed his idea of loving the neighbor "in God" like this: "Whatever or whoever is loveable to us is to be carried along to the place to which the whole torrent of our love rushes."[4] This concept is one for which modern people feel great animosity; it diminishes, discounts, and devalues the other, it's felt, to love her/him "in God." I want to suggest to you that the measure of our failure to understand this concept is exactly the measure of our notorious failure in our most pressing project — relationship. The traditional interpretations of loving the neighbor in God, the interpretations that we have inherited, and are rightly repelled by, are either that we should love the other only because he/she has a secondary, participated value in God, or we should love him/her because this is our route to reward and happiness. I am convinced that these are distortions of what Augustine was saying. Let me try to describe what he meant, not as an exercise in exegesis, but because I think it's a way of grasping something crucially important about fears of separateness and about relationship.

Augustine speaks from a world view that assumes a center

of being, of value, and of reality that the individual has access to only through her personal center. This isn't terribly
mysterious or abstract. What Augustine is claiming is that
there is something which an individual knows only through
gathering her/his most insightful self-knowledge and dwelling with it, and violates only at the expense of her own richness of being. This dwelling-with, and steadily bodying forth
in activity in the world one's treasure of self-understanding,
Augustine called "relationship to God." We can also call it
aloneness, the place at which the external and internal
shouting voices competing for attention, with all their good —
but untimely — advice, their grade school taunts, their ra-
tionalizations, cease. But this is the place at which we are
connected. This is the important thing Augustine and many
many others were saying; the place at which we give up the
communal and the private hideouts and are alone, this — *this*
is the place at which we recognize our connectedness. The
courage to be alone? It comes from being pushed to that
place — at first most unwillingly, in suffering and terror, then
after many times, with understanding, then in peace several
times, and finally, in joy — but then forgetting and beginning
again in suffering and terror. . . .

But what about loving the other "in God"? Augustine was
saying that only when we have recognized our aloneness *and*
our connectedness, only when we dwell in this place, can we
do a decent job of loving other human beings in their aloneness and connectedness; only then are we freed from clutching the systems of relationships which require others to meet
our needs, which insist that they stand in our light so that we
can't see the separateness we fear and the fragility of these
pressured relationships. Loving the other "in God" allows us
to delight in the connected aloneness of the other.

And this too is highly important; we have become, in our time, so frightened of separateness and so painfully self-conscious in relationship that it's not too much to say that we have been ordered — organized — by pain. We ask questions about our aloneness because of pain. Several years ago I was trying to explain to a close friend who'd asked why I always wore a cross. The cross, I said, is the basic symbol of my psyche, meaning for me productive pain, pain that moves one to a new and more fruitful orientation, pain that doesn't fester and grind you down, but pain you trust to teach you something important. Productive pain, I said, is pain you learn how to use. She said, "Yes, well, but . . . what about learning through joy?"

It had not occurred to me to collect joyous experiences as learning and energy. I'd become accustomed to seeing pain as an opportunity to learn. Surely the understanding of the potential productivity of pain had been a major insight; it is a major discovery that pain is not all waste and loss. None of us is born knowing this, and the excitement of realizing it is so strong that we tend to stay with it. This can be dangerously limiting; since we expect and even trust pain, we begin to look for it, maybe even to put ourselves in situations in which it's inevitable. And then we don't take the next step — and it's a giant step — of learning by the careful observation of one's own delight, recognition of the capacity of this delight to energize and unify. What would the shape of our aloneness look like if we questioned it from the perspective of delight instead of pain? Why then, I think, it would look and feel like uniqueness, a perspective of amazing richness that no one else quite duplicates; it would also look like responsibility to give some kind of form to this uniqueness; it would look like a basis for the *enjoyment* of other human beings, which is surely the best thing we can do with and for them.

Delight is a capacity, and Abraham Maslow has said that a capacity is a need. This means that a person needs to be very attentive to his/her delight and to the objects that this delight spontaneously selects. Capacities that have no freedom to actualize in work and love are needs that are not met. "Delight orders the soul,"[5] said Augustine—just a description! There is in delight a unification of the person and a reshuffling of what's important, and in shared delight a connectedness with other human beings that mirrors the quality of spontaneity and beauty that we have learned to expect in our place of connected aloneness.

In conclusion I'd like to entertain what this idea of connected aloneness might do for—or to—our ideas of "singleness" and "marriage." First, what might this "courage to be alone" mean out of marriage? I'll be very practical here: It helps me with the most pressing difficulties of living alone to understand myself as primarily constituted at the place at which I am most alone and therefore most connected, rather than to see myself as the sum of my activities and relationships and dependent on these for my self-image.

The first of these difficulties is the internalized voices I mentioned earlier, the voices that comfort or cajole or scoff at me, reteaching, perhaps, the class I taught that day and *this time* getting it right! These voices, which pass themselves off as so integral to the self and so omniscient, are not to be found in the place of connected aloneness. And so it's right to refuse the voices that paralyze and frustrate. And the self-talk that bolsters and inflates is equally illegitimate; I can't tell myself that I'm just super, that I'm "noble," or that I'm "the true Christ" as recently a young man on the subway advised me loudly all the way from Park Street to Harvard Square. Since none of these voices seems necessary or absolute any longer, since I am neither the helpless victim of whatever internalized voices I have accumulated, nor of the exaggerated megalomania that attempts to compensate for condemning voices, I can choose the voice that balances and affirms me— sometimes the voice of an adult friend, sometimes the soothing mother, sometimes the father who wants me to do a good job. I can freely select the most productive voice for the situation in which I find myself.

The other difficulty of living alone is that no one person is continuously available to remove my experience of ambiguity. There is no one when I go home every day to whom I can present an amazingly homogeneous picture, convincing to both of us, of myself as an all-reasonable, all good-intending, lovable and worthwhile person. Therefore I become painfully aware of my ambiguity, the relativity of my opinions, my actions, of my scholarly work, and the characteristic forms of deficit being that emerge in my interaction with others—eagerness to please, laziness, stubbornness. The experience of connected aloneness helps me to accept my inevitable ambiguity, modifies my dismay that I haven't learned more, faster, and balances this dismay with gratitude and delight for what I *am* learning, for the rhythmic process of learning.

And in marriage? Connected aloneness redistributes the weight so that it is not all on one point and so that a relationship of two very human beings can breathe, so that each can see the other as infinitely dear, infinitely valuable, but not as an object of infinite longing. It relieves each person of the requirement that she and he continuously reflect the "good face" of the other—as illustrated in the eighteenth-century painting by Tiepolo of the sorceress Armida and the Knight Rinaldo: The sorceress holds a mirror up for the knight; he, gazing into the mirror, falls in love with her. It helps to cut the obsessive quality of narcissism that threatens the model of marriage as mutual therapy. This model was described to me by a friend who was getting a divorce because "We simply aren't *healing* each other." It helps also to cut the idolatrous character of "romantic love" built on what Ernest Becker has called "the hunger and passion of everyone for a *localized stimulus* that takes the place of the whole world."[6]

Awareness and affirmation of — and gratitude and delight in — the connected aloneness of each of us give us the courage to be alone. I should like to give you in closing the last stanza of T. S. Eliot's "Ash Wednesday" as the finest statement about connected aloneness I know:

Blessed sister, holy mother, spirit of the fountain,
*   spirit of the garden,*
Suffer us not to mock ourselves with falsehood
Teach us to care and not to care
Teach us to sit still
Even among these rocks.
Our peace in his will
And even among these rocks
Sister, mother,
And spirit of the river, spirit of the sea.
Suffer me not to be separated
And let my cry come unto Thee.[7]

NOTES

1. Sheldon Vanauken, *A Severe Mercy* (San Francisco: Harper and Row, 1977), Ch. 2, "The Shining Barrier," *passim*.

2. Edward O. Wilson, *On Human Nature* (Cambridge, MA: Harvard University Press, 1978), p. 122.

3. Plotinus, *Ennead* VI.5.7.

4. *De doctrina christiana* I.22.

5. *De musica* VI.11.29.

6. Ernest Becker, *The Denial of Death* (New York: The Free Press, 1973), p. 147.

7. T. S. Eliot, "Ash Wednesday," *Collected Poems 1906–1962* (London: Faber and Faber Limited, 1963), p. 98.

CHAPTER 5

The Feminine Dimension of Contemplation *
🍎 Wendy M. Wright

A number of years ago, on the occasion of a religious com-
memoration, I composed a piece in which I attempted
to describe in visual terms an experience of spiritual importance that had occurred to me. I depicted myself as a traveler — a man — who was entering into himself, beginning a journey of great peril that would take him into the complex re-
gions of the inner world, through the intricacies of the mind
and the conflicting voices of self. This world was a dark labyrinth, obscure and peopled with shadowy illusions. I wondered where this traveler was being led. Into what interior
chamber of myself would he finally emerge? To my surprise
his travels did not end inside himself. Instead, the landscape
he had been traveling opened out onto a vast and peaceful
plain over which arched a star-filled night sky. I knew that

* The Christian nature of this article is stressed not necessarily to exclude other religious traditions from the remarks made but to indicate that the contemplative process is found and undergone only within the framework of some symbolic system.
While the human capacity for interiority and contemplation may be universal, any
individual journey can only be realized within a particular cultural matrix. A culture does not merely give its contemplatives a vocabulary in which to clothe their experiences but gives those experiences a certain structure and goal. Thus a Christian
contemplative journey is not necessarily identical to the interior pilgrimage of a

this place was no longer inside myself. Nor was I outside myself in the way I had been before the journey began. I was, rather, on the other side of myself—so deeply within myself that I had emerged into a transpersonal realm. I was standing on the edge of eternity. Just beyond the horizon was the mysterious center of all that is. And standing there, I recognized myself as a woman, as Mary, the bridge and Mother of God.[1]

The emergence of the figure of Mary in this psychic imagery has for some time compelled and fascinated me. It has caused me to reflect on the role of this woman—this particularly Christian image of woman—in the interior journey. Throughout the history of Christian contemplative literature, Mary has appeared as the image of the soul in its ideal relationship to God. She has been held up as the model for contemplative prayer by Bernard of Clairvaux and François de Sales. She is patroness of that great order of contemplatives, the Cistercians, and her image has inspired and instructed many writers in other monastic orders. There has long been an historical identification with the Virgin and the Christian contemplative tradition. But I have wondered,

---

Buddhist or Jew for the simple reason that a Christian has a different understanding not only of what the ultimate Reality might be but, more importantly, a different conception of what the interior landscape is like. Even within traditions themselves there are differing views of the dynamics of contemplation. For a Christian informed by Augustinian psychology, the journey is essentially voluntaristic, the will being the dominant interior faculty and love the essential motive force, the growth of which results in a growing likeness to God. For others in the tradition, the intellect is the more important faculty and divine likeness evaluated more in terms of intellectual enlightenment, while growth is seen to proceed from the rational faculties that effect the transformation of the rest of the person. Resulting different anticipations and experiences of the contemplative drama can only be expected from different self-understandings. This, I feel, does not detract from what may be a transcultural human intuition but, rather, gives full value to the very humanness of contemplation which, to use a Christian term, is profoundly incarnational.

what is the basis for this identification, and is there any in-
trinsic connection between Mary and the interior life beyond
(yet including) her function as the historical Mother of Jesus:
Is there any connection between her as feminine principle
and the life of contemplation? Further, I have wondered
what the relationship is, if there is any, to the fact of being a
woman engaged in the contemplative life and this association
of Mary and contemplation. The following is an attempt to
explore these issues.

For the Christian the contemplative experience is not one
of many experiences available to be explored and savored,
but *the* most profound experience within which all others can
be located. The contemplative experience is a centering and
centered seeing, a seeing that proceeds from the heart as well
as the mind and perceives the person in his relatedness to all
things, including himself. Through the contemplative eye
humankind is known in its harmonious relationship to the divine and to the world. In this relational seeing a knowledge is
found that can more truly be called love, for it is a knowledge
that cannot be gained independently of the experience of the
depths of love. It is a knowledge of the vital principle of relatedness — love — that binds all things, the principle that is the
internal dynamic of the Godhead itself.

The road that leads to this contemplative vision is long and
paradoxically solitary. It is a road that, taking us deeply into
ourselves, confronts us with ourselves, and thus it is an undertaking in self-analysis, an encounter with our unique psy-
chologies — our habits of mind, our emotional strengths and
weaknesses, our fears and secret hopes. But the Christian
contemplative life asks more of us than this introspection. It
asks us to probe beyond ourselves, deeper within ourselves to

a life within that is not our own. We are asked to go beyond psychology to the life of God within. This brings me back to the image of the plain beneath the night sky. There, on the other side of ourselves, we are faced with a reality that speaks to us of the immensity of what it is to be human. There we stand at the sacred threshold where all beginnings and ends find their source.

Beneath the night sky, standing on the threshold of eternity, is a woman, Mary. I do no think the occurrence of this image is accidental; rather, it is full of meaning. We are each of us composed of many facets. We each have within ourselves the capacity for agency — the drive and perseverance to assert ourselves, to carry out our plans and desires, to change the world around us through action. Likewise, we have the capacity for receptivity — the ability to accept and wait upon life, to be informed and changed by the worlds around and within us. One way to envision ourselves is as beings possessing these two principles of agency and receptivity. St. Augustine, one of the fathers of the Christian contemplative tradition, called these principles *superbia* (power) and *humilitas* (humility), and construed the central task of the Christian to be the surrender to the life of *humilitas,* which is the spiritual life, and the relinquishment of the life of *superbia,* the worldly life. We could also refer to these principles of agency or lack of agency as the masculine and feminine parts of ourselves. Our masculine selves are agential, our feminine selves receptive.

These designations may cause some people difficulties. A talented, self-directed career woman may feel as though I am saying that all females are essentially passive, pliant creatures created to bear children and be the helpmates of men. Nothing could be further from the truth. I am using masculine

and feminine as evocative terms that can aid us in conceptu-
alizing our inner dynamics. Also — and this is primarily why I
choose to employ them — these terms have correspondence to
the images found in religious iconography. Thus, if we are
going to attempt to read the images of Christianity in a creative, living way — read them as if they had meaning not only
in an historical sense but in an allegorical or mystical sense —
we must allow the images of women or men to sometimes
have interior referents. We must be able to identify ourselves,
or facets of ourselves, as participants in an inner drama that
can be visually depicted. We must allow our spiritual journey
to be expressed in the living symbols given to us through religious tradition.

So we return once again to Mary standing beneath the
dark sky. For our purposes here, I will interpret her as the
feminine aspect of ourselves, and the earlier male figure of
the inner journey as the masculine dimension. Thus, reading
the whole drama as the story of the contemplative life, we can
see *that* life as a dynamic interaction of the masculine and
feminine sides of ourselves. We must assume the masculine
role, we must make a journey, we must consciously gather the
scattered fragments of ourselves and set out upon the inner
path. In the process we must act, we must choose, we must be
agential. Christian tradition gives us the terminology for this
activity: It is understood that we must mortify ourselves, discipline ourselves, choose good over evil, judge the outer fruits
of our inner desire for God, purify ourselves — in short, the
contemplative life is a life of transformation, of perpetual
change. It exists and is realized *in time,* and must conform to
the shifting, active dynamics of time.

But the contemplative experience, though realized in time,
is also timeless. We sometimes break through ourselves to

find ourselves beyond time. Here we can no longer assert our agency. For the posture we must assume in the presence of this mystery is not upright, not agential, but kneeling and receptive to the awesome life before us. As we progress in the contemplative life, this dimension unfolds more and more so that the masculine side is eclipsed, allowing our receptivity to realize its potential. We become the feminine, become Mary. Like Mary we wait, a yes on our lips, yet unknowing. Open, responsive to the transcendent reality within, we are made ready to hear and embrace the divine Word. There, on the threshold of eternity we become intimate to the conception of divine Love.

So it is possible to visualize the contemplative life in terms of the masculine and feminine capacities in people. But so far I have used these terms very generally as being descriptive of a spiritual process. Can they be used to help us envision the psychological dynamics of the contemplative experience? I should pause here. Some people may be confused by the distinction made between psychology and spirituality (although I alluded to this earlier). Certainly the contemplative journey, from the point of view of the individual especially, cannot be conceived apart from one's own unique psychology. Any spirituality that claims to exist apart from concrete experience or pretends to bypass the human would seem to run the risk of being illusory or meaningless. Psychological data must always be an important part of the spiritual life. But I think that one cannot equate spirituality and psychology. For then one would be in danger of reducing the experience of the transcendent within to merely an activity of mind and one would be tempted to explain it in limited psychological language. Certainly the testimony of the great Christian contemplatives would refute this view. Of course, it is possible to construct a psychology (I am thinking of C. G. Jung particularly) that would allow room for at least the possibility of a transpersonal element. But as much help as traditional psychological theory can be in the clarification of self, it alone is not enough to explore the farthest limits of what it is to be human.

Having said that, perhaps it is time to investigate further what the terms masculine and feminine might mean in the psychology of the inner life. Two separate insights shared with me have given me the opportunity to muse on this. First, it was related to me that the venerable prior of a contemplative monastery described the contemplative life as "a discovery of the feminine within," and then added that this, at least, is true for men; he didn't know about women. Secondly, the feminist theologian, Naomi R. Goldenberg, in her book *Changing of the Gods*, expanding on the ideas of other feminist theologians, explores the possibility that since Western theology has been written primarily by men, its insights into the nature of reality are particularly male. For instance, in the formulation of the concept of sin, theologians have dealt with only those sinful dispositions particular to males — the will to power or arrogant self-assertion — yet they have generalized these concepts to include females. The feminist theologians want to suggest that there are sinful dispositions more inherently female that center on the problem of the underdevelopment or negation of self (for example, the lack of an organizing center, or dependence on others for one's self-definition). These two insights raise the question: Is the psychology of the contemplative experience the same for men and women?

St. Paul would claim that in Christ there is neither male

nor female. In Christ, I believe this is true. But in ourselves we are female or male, we are not born neuter. We may be spiritually *reborn* in Christ, but we are born only to die and rise again, time after time. This, at any rate, is the teaching of the Christian mystics. Incorporation in the mystical body of Christ may begin with baptism but it does not end there. A deeper and deeper assimilation and transformation occurs only through time. Further, this assimilation does not obliterate our personalities. In a very profound sense we will always be who we are, and who we are is either male or female.

I would like to return now to the image of the woman beneath the night sky, keeping in mind the question just posed: Is the psychology of the contemplative experience the same for men and women? This starlit image shows us, I believe, the general pattern of the contemplative journey. The masculine principle of agency prepares the way for and then relinquishes its place to the feminine principle of receptivity. The question is: Do women find themselves in the same relationship to these interior masculine and feminine principles as men do? My intuition, spurred on by the intuition of the prior and the feminist theologians, tells me no. Most women (I would not say all women, some women might fit more comfortably into another pattern) are more essentially identified with their feminine selves than their masculine selves. By biology and upbringing (for there is a cultural component in this too) they are more deeply attached to the feminine principle and tend to develop their nurturing and receptive sides. I would also like to suggest, and this again is based on intuition, that on some deeper level than biology or culture, woman directly receives her identity from a source or femininity beyond herself. She belongs to this source in a way that a man cannot, for he does not embody, does not incarnate, the feminine in himself.

The embodiment of the feminine. Physically, emotionally, mentally a woman. How could such a person stand in the same relationship to the feminine element of the contemplative life as does a man, for whom the feminine is essentially the *other*? The prior may be correct in saying that the discovery of the feminine within constitutes the contemplative experience of a man. But what is this same experience for a woman? If she is so essentially connected to the source of receptivity, is she then more suited for the contemplative life, by nature already attuned to the receptivity that that life requires? Of course not. Neither sex is by nature more equipped for the contemplative journey. We are all of us outside ourselves, needing to enter into ourselves in order to go beyond ourselves. But I think that the psychological preparation for and undertaking of that journey is quite different for a woman than for a man.

We return once more to the modern feminist theologians and their notion of female sins. These sins relate to the underdevelopment of self and are described as the lack of an organizing center or focus, dependence on others for one's self-definition, triviality, distractability and diffuseness. These sinful dispositions appear to be caricatures of a feminine receptivity that has degenerated into an unconscious passivity. They are the feminine lulled into weakness or aimlessness, having failed to realize its possible strength. Just as masculine agency untempered by any other influences can swell into an overbearing will to power, so feminine receptivity left unassisted is susceptible to selflessness. Each principle seems to need the enlivening influence of the other.

This being so, can it then be said that for a woman the contemplative journey consists in the realization of her essential nature through the cultivation of the *otherness* in her; through the cultivation of her agency, her masculine capacity for focus, clarity, action, discipline, and order? Yes, I think this is true, with one emphatic qualification. A woman embarking on the inner quest is not calling upon the resources of her masculine side in order to develop her agency for its own sake. She is not becoming more conscious of her self as an individual solely for the purpose of becoming less dependent on others for her sense of self. Instead, she is discovering her masculine side in order that it may help her to articulate, define and direct who she essentially is. Her masculine self can help her become conscious of her true nature, of the deep and fecund wells of the feminine within. In the delicate yet radical disclosure of this nature she is informed by the other within herself.

Perhaps the images of Mary that emerge from Christian tradition can teach us something about this particular female disclosure of the feminine within. Mary, traditionally, has been seen as the paradigm of the human soul in its ideal relationship to God. If I may allow myself some creative seeing, I would like to look at some of Mary's images anew in light of the issues I have just explored. Mary will become the model of a woman's soul seized and carried by the contemplative impulse. Her story will become the story of a woman—deeply identified with her feminine self and perceiving her masculine self as "other"—on her inner journey. True to the Christian model of the contemplative life she will find within her a transcendent dimension that radically transforms her. What begins as an exploration in personal psychology becomes a predominantly spiritual process. Gaining access to the deepest center of her soul, she discovers the power within that fashions her human potential in exquisite responsiveness to the divine touch.

The story begins before the Gospel accounts in the Hebrew Bible's *Song of Songs.* In this love poem, interpreted by many Christian mystics as the song of the contemplative soul, the bride-to-be longs for union with her bridegroom, seeking him as the soul seeks its happiness and fulfillment in union with God. The *Song of Songs* is a story of courtship, of desire, of the unwedded woman awaiting her beloved. She is still daughter, not yet having become wife or mother. The feminine lacks the "other," is still seeking him. She is not yet Mary, not yet the chosen spouse. She is the unnamed, undifferentiated feminine. Not until she is led to the bridal chamber will she know who she is, will she be initiated into the meaning of her feminine identity. Not until she knows her bridegroom will she know her name, the name that contains within itself the mystery of her destiny.

It is in the Gospels that this destiny becomes clear. We see Mary, a young affianced woman receiving a startling and disquieting message from an angelic visitor. She hears his words — that she will bear a child — in a spirit of perplexed yet willing acceptance. Thy will be done, she says, although I do not understand how this can be nor what it may mean for me. In this poignant moment Mary becomes the embodiment of the soul acquiescing to the indwelling of God. She allows herself to be possessed by, to be made a bride of, God. In her act of surrender of what is most intimate to her — her very life — she received within herself the life of God. I have always been struck by the fact that at the Annunciation an angel — a male angel — is present. The angel is not the gift Mary is to receive, nor does he bring the gift. Rather, he *informs* her of what is occurring within her in a much deeper and more interior way. Can we read this image creatively and say that, in a woman, the mysterious penetration of God occurs almost unconsciously, deep within the womb of the feminine itself, and that a woman is made conscious of this entering by her masculine guide. Without his annunciation, she could not freely assent to the divine will, could not truly cooperate in the plan designed for her. Without his knowledge the love conceived within her could not joyously be brought to birth.

Mary waits patiently nine long months. The feminine, true to its own nature, bears patiently, allows life to grow within it, gives of its own substance to form what is emerging from it. The divine seed is planted and takes shape within. The shape it assumes is of a male-child, a child yet at the same time God. Perhaps what Mary is bearing is the masculine inextricably joined to the divine will, her own agency animated by the transcendent agency of God.

She brings it joyously to birth. And it is a Virgin Birth — Virgin not only because it is an interior and spiritual birth, but because in the process of conceiving and bringing forth this divine child, Mary's original innocence has not been lost. Her profoundly feminine nature has not been violated or disturbed, the integrity of her feminine receptivity has not been compromised. For the secret entering of the divine life is in complete harmony with her own true nature, as is the emergence of the other from her very depths, for Mary's assent to both of these events *is* the feminine. At the Annunciation and the Nativity she manifests her SELF most fully: poised on the sacred threshold that delimits the human and divine, she is taken in the intimate embrace of divinity and made partner in creation itself.

Virgin. But also mother. Paradoxically, yet with absolute appropriateness, this innocence flowers. The feminine, still Virgin, is brought into a fuller realization of its own nature, is initiated into the ways of its maturity and is taught the deep springs of its own feminine life. We see now Madonna and child. Now Mary learns a receptivity different from a daughter's obedience, different from a bride's desire. She learns an attentiveness, a responsiveness to the growing God-man in her care. She simultaneously learns from him, from the developing other, and is forced back upon her own resources to discover new depths within herself. Her capacity to wait upon, to serve yet not be servile, to bear both sorrow and joy is increased over and over again as she cares for her son.

Mary is aware of this child's true calling; she knows where he rightly belongs. So she brings him to the Temple, an offering to God. We see her at the Presentation holding out her infant to the high priest — the feminine making conscious acknowledgment of the rightful disposition of her masculine side. This male child will serve the divine life within him, will follow to the end the destiny that will lead him to that goal. And because she has given birth to and will raise him, Mary is told that she too will suffer, a sword will pierce her side as well. She, the essential feminine, will participate in, be wounded and transformed by, the passion awaiting the God principle now shaping the focus of her life.

As the child in her care moves beyond infancy "growing in wisdom," Mary's individual story becomes absorbed in and eclipsed by the story of her son. Can this mean that the feminine becomes at the same time less obviously central to the woman's contemplative journey and yet that this feminine must assume a new aspect, must actualize its mature potential by becoming the embodiment of silent waiting upon the will of God? I think so. She is no longer called upon to guide the immature Christ child toward his destiny but must allow him to assume control, experiencing her own destiny more clearly through the emergence of his mysterious calling. The focus is now upon the masculine, upon Christ. He, a woman's agency divinely informed, becomes central to the development of the story.

The state of the woman engaged in the contemplative life is reflected in the traditional paradigms. Her essential feminine self waits upon, silently encourages the "other" within whose maturity allows him to know of and carry out his divinely directed mission. He guides her in a life of discipline, self-surrender, charity and increasing active assimilation into a God-centered existence. There are not many biblical or legendary images of Mary to inform us of the feminine's role and development during the period of Jesus' ministry. The focus is upon the now tremendously creative and compelling unfolding of the masculine within.

Nonetheless, something subtle is occurring within the depths of the feminine at this time. Through the development of the son the mother is becoming readied to be bride once again. It is coincidental perhaps, but nonetheless evocative that during the period of Jesus's ministry we encounter Mary and her son at a marriage feast in Cana. The wine has run out. Mary informs Jesus of the fact and he miraculously transforms water into wine. Mary assists by directing the servants to pour: "Do as he tells you," she says. We view the feminine present at a marriage feast at which the masculine symbolically unveils the meaning of the mystic union to be achieved through his own death and resurrection. A mystic marriage awaits the feminine on the contemplative journey. Her marriage will be the mysterious and intimate initiation into the very life of the Godhead itself. The woman whose inner journey is thus depicted can be seen as having been initiated into the depths of the contemplative experience to the extent that she no longer calls her life her own. God himself now lives and acts within. Union is achieved.

But the passage into this union is a passage through death. The first to die is the masculine principle, which had so recently achieved its full human potential. We see Mary at the foot of the Cross receiving the anguish to which she, through her son's destiny, was destined. The masculine must die in its human dimension in order to be taken up into the Godhead to complete its ordained course. It must be completely assimilated into the divine principle by which it has been guided, it must transcend its own human limitations and surrender to the agency of God alone. The feminine must endure this as well. She must lose what has become dearer to her than her own life. She must let go of her agency, surrender it to an awful and incomprehensible fate. Only then can what has been a psychological process—inspired as it may have been—reveal itself in its transcendent fullness. A woman's masculine agency is transformed by and into an agency outside itself.

The traditional images show us that for a woman the principle of masculine agency within must first assume a dominant role, then die to itself and be resurrected in a new and spiritual body. The feminine principle, as a psychological entity, remains, transformed in that it is no longer undifferentiated or incapable of discipline and ethical action, but it still awaits a deeper knowledge, a more radical intimacy with the transcendent that so long ago addressed and claimed it for its own.

Once again, the feminine must wait. It must grow and mature, readying itself for a final union. But it does not wait alone. Mary is present at the time of Pentecost, when the fiery spirit of the risen Christ is transmitted to the disciples. In this final period of expectancy, the feminine will be guided not by the man who was once her own child but by the transcendent spirit that he sends.

The waiting ends once again in death, Mary's own. Her death, like her son's, is to be a rebirth. The traditional iconography of the Dormition of the Virgin expresses this in a moving and tender way. The deceased Madonna lies upon her bed, the disciples gathered around her, while above her her son, in his glory, receives her soul now in the form of an infant into his arms. As she once cradled him, now he cradles her. She is reborn into the life of the risen God.

The final transformation of the feminine principle from a psychological into a spiritual reality is depicted in the exquisite images of the Assumption and the Coronation. After her death, Mary, mother of Jesus, is gathered up, body and soul, into heaven. There she is met by the Trinity itself, which invests her with the symbol of her eternal dominion — the crown — and grants her her new identity and name, Queen of Heaven. Here, in the womb of the Godhead itself, the feminine is reborn to the life to which it was destined. She joins her regnant Son as consort, as bride. At his side she rules, masculine and feminine now transformed beyond and for all time.

It is from this transfigured union of male and female that the ripe fruits of the contemplative life come. Mary, the mother of Jesus, takes on a new significance once she has joined her heavenly spouse. She becomes the Mother of the Faithful, the Intercessor between man and God. Her part in the redemption of the world is not limited to the historical events of her life, as extraordinary as these might have been. She becomes, rather, a living bridge between heaven and earth. With maternal solicitude she reaches down into the depths of human ignorance and offers the nourishment of her wisdom. And with infinite compassion she receives the prayer of the faithful, bearing them gently into the presence of the divine judgment, swaddling their imperfections in the mantle of her concern.

So too, a woman's now transformed feminine self bears fruit. With its long-tested relationship with its masculine counterpart serving as background, the feminine realizes its fullest potential and achieves in a woman her deepest flowering. At once active and contemplative, this whole woman now shares the discoveries of her inner quest with others. She becomes a living channel for the inflowing of the divine presence into the world and a translucent window through which the radiance of that presence can be viewed.

NOTES

1. This particular imagery, as suggested, had a complex genesis. Its nucleus was a single dream image which became visually expanded through the analytical use of active imagination. Its further implications were only realized in prayer during which (over a prolonged period of time) the unapparent meanings of the symbols emerged. Finally, it was conscious literary effort combined with creative receptivity that brought the piece to birth.

CHAPTER 6

The Sexual Mystic: Embodied Spirituality

🍎 *Dorothy H. Donnelly*

> Every act and gesture is a word spoken. We are not overspiritualizing our view of sex when we say that every sexual act, feeling, or emotion has the power to become a disclosure of spirit to spirit. Sexuality is never something by itself. It is always meaning incarnate.[1]
>
> *D. D. Williams*

"Feminist" and "mystic"! They may seem worlds apart in popular parlance, but in the interpretations found in this collection, how truly complementary. Mary Giles's integration and definition of these terms in expanded connotations is overdue. One fundamental basis for that integration lies in the unity of the human person that woman is. The appelation "feminist" mystic restores woman to her birthright —full humanity and integrated spirituality. Upon her shoulders thereby is laid the responsibility for reinterpreting human experience through female eyes for a world nauseous from thousands of years of a one-sided male approach to reality.

Out of male-dominated sciences and arts came our present

philosophy, theology, psychology and sociology. Rare indeed were the women who could pass through the academic mills and emerge with undamaged self-concepts, so invisible was women's impact on curricula. Yet, today, in a splendid reversal, women professors challenge women students and recover and transmit valid female experience caught through the sensitive radar of the female body, mind and spirit.

Dualism stood always in the female path as chief obstacle to confidence in her own experience, for both church and society had taught women (and men) a denigratory view of the body as inferior to the soul. So flight from the body had become synonymous with the pursuit of the spirit, and the goal: to be alone with the Alone, rejecting the suspect body as evil and an embarrassing companion in that pursuit.

This dualistic split between body and spirit had roots in both paganism and Christianity with bizarre consequences for women. The Old Testament saw women as sexual objects, as property listed before the husband's other possessions in Deuteronomy (5:21), but after his house in Exodus. Across centuries women had become associated with the material, then, the nonspiritual, the sexual, and consequently, the ritually impure. Intercourse with women could render impure a priest who was scheduled for worship in the Temple.

As the Hebrews had fought the pagan goddesses, so the Jewish converts to Christianity had to struggle with the devotees of the Egyptian Isis and the Phrygian Magna Mater whose cults were all pervasive: "The most effective rival to Christianity from the second century onward, and during the temporary revival of classical paganism in Rome (A.D. 394) was the cult of Isis; it was her festival that was celebrated with great magnificence."[2]

Women, then, not only represented all that was bodily,

and therefore "inferior," but cults like those of Isis, considered an aberration by the early church, also intensified Christian repugnance to the sight of women in worship. Soon Christianity boasted an all-male clergy and women lost any gains made in the first two centuries through the teaching of Jesus. The prevalent Graeco-Roman culture, permeated with anti-feminism, finally triumphed in the nascent church. The most influential spiritual leaders and theologians fulminated against women: "You are the door of Satan; you are the one that yielded to the temptation of the tree; you are the first deserter of the law of God; you persuaded man whom Satan himself had not power to subdue; with irresponsibility you led man, the image of God, astray!"[3]

Behind pagan and Christian scorn of women lay deep roots of superstition and ignorance. Men, puzzled by women's biological processes, resorted to magic or demon possession for explanations for menstruation, pregnancy and the power to conceive. From such explanations came woman's connection with the dark, dangerous and ultimately with the "evil" dimensions of life. Soon, by some strange psychological nuance, "evil" became morally evil as well. Woman's inferiority was now translated as spiritual incompetence.

Gnostic dualism, Greek philosophy, and cultic purity conceptions, even the encratism that forbade marriage as evil—all of these fused for Christians into an obsession with anti-sexuality as inimical to spiritual living. As Rosemary Haughton aptly states:

> The Christian teaching about the new life in Christ into which the believer entered by faith but which would be fully established when the world and the flesh (meaning all that is unredeemed and blind in human nature) would be overcome, did lend itself to an interpretation

and emphasized the *rejection of physical experience
and pleasure,* even of beauty, and the exaltation of the
spiritual, here meaning the nonphysical.[4]

Out of this rejection of the physical came anti-sexual mea-
sures like the law of celibacy for clergy, which was meant to
show their superiority to pagan and Jewish priests. Soon,
monasteries required a vow of celibacy and the "spiritual life"
was henceforth identified with the nonmaterial, nonphysical, the disembodied — which meant, paradoxically, the totally male.

By the fourth century this antisexual obsession triumphed
in the works of the finest theologians of the West. St. Jerome
could only see hope for woman in becoming a man; St. Augustine of Hippo, whose thinking would constitute the bulk
of theology for a thousand years, taught that original sin
passed on to children through the act of conception itself.

Many fled to the monasteries for spiritual living; others, to
avoid disastrous ecomonic conditions, but many, too, fled
the problem that sexuality had become. Yet many women
found in those same monasteries the dawn of liberation from
the stigma society attached to the female body. Melania the
Elder, Paula and Eustochium found in monasticism a cultural and intellectual option that shines out in their correspondence. Women's spiritual life blossomed in the deserts where
some 20,000 nuns resided at one time — in comparison to
10,000 monks.

But married women of all ranks now found themselves
identified with Eve's sin in the Genesis myth as that story became the central explanation of human evil. Holiness had
become synonymous with abstention from sex, and because
prayer demanded such abstinence in the eyes of the Fathers

of the Church, priests called to sanctity could never marry. Studies like those of Samuel Laeuchli[5] give detailed explications of these developments. Here, we only attempt a thumbnail sketch of the complex movements that combined to produce the dualistic antifeminism only now beginning to fade in church and society.

The half-Christianized medieval period certainly created no new theology to change women's inferior position. Ignorance and long-standing custom only deepened it, if anything. The legitimacy of prostitution as a social institution appeared in Gregory the Great, Isidore of Seville and in St. Thomas (d. 1274), who called the prostitute "a sewer in the palace," a "lawful immorality"[6] as a necessary evil. This acceptance of social aberrations was typical of both pagan and Christian religions and continues in East and West to this day. Only Mary's role as Mother of God whom Jesus obeyed led medieval men to find it no dishonor to obey a French queen like Blanche or the famed abbesses of Las Huelgas in Spain.

The Renaissance and Reformation revived Greek ideas about woman's inferiority and reversed the medieval acceptance above, so much so that we find the monks of Fontevrault in 1636 rebelling against their abbess because now the age found it dishonorable, since it was "against nature" for a male to obey a woman. They further contended that such obedience would be against "God's law."[7] Neither Luther nor Calvin carried out for women the liberation from decadent theology they tried to gain for men. Some of the first changes in Christian communities blossomed on American soil and produced some degree of women's religious-sexual equality. Some groups chose her as their leader and gave her ordination or its equivalent: the Quakers under George Fox, certain tenets of the Oneida Community and the Shakers under Mother Anna Lee.[8]

Today women are called upon to transform that painful story and reclaim our total humanity through, rather than in spite of, being embodied as females, as coequally responsible with males for the fate of this planet. We are learning and creating a broader definition of "sexuality." No longer confined to the single act of genital intercourse, sexuality is the energy of our relating as women to everyone and everything. We as sexual beings must think through, theologize and philosophize about the meaning of our sexuality and employ it as the ambiance of any spirituality we may wish to live. We must develop an integrated humanity by recovering sexuality as a value, a gift and a basis for healthy spirituality.

The false dichotomy between body and spirit cannot be allowed to endure. Any discussion of sex and spirit must take into account the life of the spirit, mind *and* body as the way we relate to God, self and others through the prism of faith. For too many women, unfortunately, the myth of a divided spirituality survives, and too often it is equated with that antisexuality rampant in the ancient world. There are two reasons for this distressing association. The first has to do with the poor self-image we have inherited from the negative conditioning suffered throughout the history of Christianity. The second is the anthropomorphic concept of God as an asexual, timeless being uninvolved in our world. Under this double burden dualism marches on and continues to shape the spiritual inferiority complex of countless women.

We can counter the myth of a divided spirituality by reclaiming a history of women's experience and emphasizing a theology that centers on ourselves and God as beings who relate one with another. It is not enough to do only the first, for the spirituality of each women is understood in large part through theology. If the self-concept is the single most important component of our behavior, including our spiritual liv-

ing, then women, with centuries of conditioning about inferior spiritual capabilities, now must fight back and liberate
ourselves from the mythology and inadequate theology that
deprive God of meaning and ourselves of expectations of
sanctity.

In reclaiming our own experience, we see clearly that authentic spirituality must be eminently social. Women as persons exist in openness to others; indeed that is the very meaning of person. We pursue a thou, even if the search for the ultimate Thou be unconscious. We do experience trying to go
beyond the ego, yearning for meaning and belonging, wanting reverence and revelation. If religion is "the audacious attempt to conceive of the entire universe as humanly meaningful,"[9] then women must now claim our own meaning in terms
of the experience of relating and thus contribute to revital-
izing religion as well as other social institutions.

History has shown us women whose mystic experience in
what I call the "mystic circle" moved from contemplative
prayer as learning love into intensive social involvement. Teresa of Avila and Catherine of Siena reveal this circle in the
preparatory periods of their lives where God teaches the
woman who and what she is and can be. Then, in a magnificent spiral of ever-increasing love, she moves out into the
marketplace, civil or religious, but in a new mode of operation. Now she is empowered through her embodied spirituality rather than in spite of it. Her cultural milieu may fight the
idea of God's love penetrating spirit *and* body, but her experience is irrefutable, and she continues her work for others,
climbing over mountains of obstacles with incredible ease—
and incredible pain.

Valid mystical feminism reaches out, then, to our neighbor; it is social, rooted in love and ablaze with concern. Cath-

erine of Genoa, who could say in mystical hyperbole, "My Being *is* God, not by some simple participation but by a true transformation of my being,"[10] finished her life as an administrator of the famous Pammatone Hospital for the sick poor of Genoa. All the while she supervised doctors, nurses and complex details of organizations and cared for the sick during a major plague, her spiritual life and love-relationship with God deepened in passion and intensity.

In relating one to another, we employ all kinds of symbols. We signal to one another from our enclosed private worlds, hoping to convey meaning. Our language—words of love, hate, fear and joy—must journey on human breath, itself a product of human *embodiedness*, which is a term for our experience of the dimension of corporality. Any dichotomy of bodily activities on the one hand and intellectual and spiritual ones on the other is fallacious in the process of conveying meaning. We are totally sexual, for all that we do is done as woman . . . or man. We do not *have* bodies; we *are* bodies in a most real sense. The highest spiritual acts of our lives demand bodily means to express them unless we would become disembodied spirits, and then, of course, we would no longer experience *human* spirituality. To express spiritual consciousness we must employ the body, and in this sense the body is holy symbol. Ultimately, as creators and users of symbols we are ourselves, in our total being, living symbol.

The moment we commence relating socially, we enter the area of human communication and must learn to convey meaning or withdraw from the enterprise. Since every human relationship is an eternal responsibility, we experience fear and anxiety as well as joy and affirmation in such relationships. Cultural conditioning in its dualistic aspects arouses guilt and fear about the sexual aspect of our loving and being loved. Many women have settled for despising the bodily aspects of loving or seek them as a panacea for any human tension. Yet, everything we do is sexual because the body is necessarily and beautifully involved in the doing. Sexuality, then, is also the greater intercourse we enjoy with the world in and through its Creator.

The feminist mystic is sexual as she encounters God in and through her body, and her female sexuality sustains the loving encounter. Release from fear of sexuality in mystical experience is an outcome we may hope for if we recover the body as gift, as holy, as life's openness to meaning, as light, and as condition of loving and being loved.

The fear of sexuality may lessen as we replace an asexual, static, God, uninvolved in human life, with our experience of relating to a dynamic Beloved who participates in our living. The idea of God as asexual, a by-product of the damaged self-concept that refuses equal status to the body as a conveyor of spiritual meaning, is, then, the second obstacle to our integrating sexuality and spirituality.

To overcome that obstacle, let us probe the nature of loving. Over centuries the integrating power of "love" that fuses sex and spirit at high temperatures has fallen prey to theories that smack strongly of the dualistic, split-level operation. Classic distinctions used in Christian ethics, for instance, divide "love" into *eros* as longing for the beloved, *agape* as sacrificial love for God and humans, *philia* as friendship, and *libido* as sexual desire. Yet all these are aspects of the thrust to oneness of human love rather than four flavors from which to choose. All four mine the rich layers of ambiguity that in love and art make for beauty and delight.

The categorization of love has continued until recent times when Anders Nygren's quite influential work presented God's love, *agape*, as the model of Christian love, and distinguished between it and human love, or sexual passion — *eros*.[11] *Apage*, or spiritual love, had no part with yearning, passion or sexual completion. Nygren's position finds little support in the Scriptures or in the historical development of the use of these terms; it is based on Platonic dualism, Stoic approaches to virtue as absence of passion and the work of Christian theologians who were influenced by both. *Agape* and *eros* have remained divorced ever since.

A theology based on human experience opens the door to new interpretations that respect the fact that we do experience unity in our embodied selves. Sex needs *eros* or "the drive toward union with what we belong to, union with our own possibilities, union with significant others . . . in relation to whom we discover our own self-fulfillment."[12] *Philia* is never totally lacking in sexual overtones, even if no genital expression is desired, for touching, caring, embracing and longing for each other's presence is the delightful presence of *eros* in *philia*.

So also in *agape*, I believe, love is not divorced from elements of attraction, receiving, yearning, longing, self-completion. *Agape* in relation to *eros* is part of the process of expressing my love in a human way to God and to others. *Eros* and *agape* are not separate loving, one sexual, and the other spiritual; they are merely labels, now outdated, but once convenient for discerning the nuances of the thrust to wholeness which is manifested in our yearning for human or divine lover.

Spirituality for the feminist mystic, then, implies a primary relating with God that can partake of any and all four of these dimensions of human loving. Living embodied is a gift, the basis of a healthy spirituality and integrated humanity. Neither sex nor spirit is end in itself, but each is helpful partner in the enterprise of learning to give and accept love, and to experience union with others and God. Divorcing *eros* from that enterprise spells its failure, for erotic love has the power to carry us out of ourselves toward the beloved. But neither can *eros* stand alone; it needs *agape* to temper destructive tendencies that can strangle love in possessiveness, fascination, or idolatry.[13]

If we reject *eros* and *libido*, and in so doing, reject our bodies, we can no longer give ourselves freely in sexual encounter with the lover. For when we deny the gift of our own sexuality, we thereby deprive ourselves of any gift to give in love. Our response to being without a gift is to create idols out of those to whom we cling, and in such idolatry we never achieve intimacy because we bring no treasured gift of our own uniqueness for our partner.

Spirituality, then, is living our faith as human and that means embodied. It is totally involved with the art of loving, the pristine art of intergrating. Comparing *agape* love just described with Jules Toner's philosophical approach to the concept of "radical love,"[14] we can see further how love integrates sex and spirit. For Toner insists that when we love, we are present to the beloved and they, present to us, in coexistence, physically, intellectually, spiritually, with affection and passion as coforms of presence. He feels that the inclination-to-union must not be confused with union itself, a point the mystics affirms. Radical love is itself an act of being-in-union that presupposes a knowing and loving the beloved that make possible the deeper union of knowledge.

Nor will Toner as philosopher give the name of love to mere thinking-alike or learning-to-share. The "union-of-presence" that characterizes love is a participating in the life of the beloved and experiencing the beloved's life as one's own, while always remaining uniquely one's own.

An interesting psychological process takes place, however, before the mystery and miracle of union by loving presence happens. Sebastian Moore calls us to consider human love and God's love through the dynamic at work in "falling in love." When attracted to someone, I experience a desire to be "someone for them." And when the beloved knows of my attraction and responds to it with love, I experience surprise, even disbelief, and my original desire as lover moves to a new stage.[15] Moore insists that we are not talking about love as merely a feeling of one person for another; love demands the response of the other if it is to grow.

Here we see the "present with" and "present-in" described by Jules Toner, with the added dynamic: Love intensifies and is liberated in the lover when she finds out that the beloved also loves. This psychological process throws light on the profundity of St. John's statement: "God hath *first* loved us!" Once that love is accepted in a breakthrough of surprise and joy, the "good news" happens.

As we move to understanding something of God in terms of relating, this dynamic of human love provides a model of how God acts in making love to and with us. It implies, first of all, that there is within us a *capacity* for receiving that love. Every desire to go beyond self to what is true, beautiful and good is the shining out of that innate desire for God, no matter what we call it.

Toner's "radical love" also calls for participating in my beloved's life as if it were my own; and yet I remain uniquely myself. So also when I begin to let God love me, participation begins. I experience God's life as mine; the mystic process has begun. Some dimension of my personality surrenders in love to God, be it body, mind, spirit. Yet by this letting-go I am not demeaned but dignified, not lessened but fulfilled because of the quality and being of the Beloved. God, as lover, is in me as gift, as in human love. Some theologians call that gift of God's self the "Holy Spirit." And I, too, am in God, my beloved, as gift when I say "yes" to being so loved. But incredibly enough, I am in God, my Lover, as an accepted, cherished, even longed-for gift. I can give God something God lacks and wants — my love.

Do we imagine that such loving union, such living within and presence-with-and-to precludes our sexuality — or God's? Even if we do not fully understand how God relates within God's Selfhood, God, too, as lover, must have organs of relationship. This is proven in God's modes of relating to us. So we cannot separate out of God's love for us that embodiedness which our spirituality models and uses to respond to that love.

Warped as we may be by dualism, we might experience culture shock to think of God as *ensexed*, as possessed of divine means of relating analogous to the many modes we use to express our sexuality. God could hardly be deprived of such if God *is* Love and source of all delight whose nature it is to love. But I do not imagine that God would be disturbed by our fumbling attempt to acknowledge Her capacity to touch us tenderly in love in manifold ways "organically." If God is Anyone, God is clearly Lover as we see so dramatically in the annals of Western woman-mystics.

When God makes love, that loving can and often does involve bodily rapture, a delightful inebriation, an intercourse with divine love. Teresa of Avila speaks of the soul willing to be in the "paradise of delights" as it is "made one with the Lord of love . . . nor can one merit so delightful a favor from the Lord, so intimate a union or a love so destined to be experienced and felt . . . grant me this favor: Let Him kiss me with the kiss of His mouth, for without You, what am I, Lord? Now, I see, my Bridegroom, that You are mine!"[16]

Hadewijch, the Beguine mystic of the thirteenth century, goes so far as to say:

> . . . the soul is a bottomless abyss in which God suffices to himself; and his own self-sufficiency ever finds fruition in this soul to the full, as the soul, for its part, ever does in him. Soul is a way for the passage of God from his depths into his liberty; and God is a way for the passage of the soul into its liberty . . . into his inmost depths, which cannot be touched except by the soul's abyss . . . so long as God doesn't belong to her in his totality, he doesn't truly satisfy her.[17]

In perhaps the most famous of all mystical poems, John of the Cross speaks as a male human being of the heavenly Lover:

> *When the breeze blew from the turret*
> *Parting His hair,*
> *He wounded my neck*
> *With his gentle hand*
> *Suspending all my senses.*
> *I abandoned and forgot myself*
> *Laying my face on my Beloved;*
> *All things ceased; I went out from myself,*
> *Leaving my cares*
> *Forgotten among the lilies.*[18]

True mystics receive the freedom of the children of God in their bodies for these are rendezvous, the trysting place of

God and their truest selves. As one monk put it: "The sensible is the cause of the conceptual; the body is the cause of the soul and precedes it in the intellect." The body held erect in prayer, the hands to the heavens, was called the language of desire. Like "a tree in the night, without it being necessary to add the sounds of words," the soul held deepest intercourse with God.[19]

God, then, loves us sexually because God loves us as human. Embodiedness becomes the magic ring, the sacred space for the act of worship that union with God epitomizes. In that act of love, God burns away the dross, and the suffering soul is afire with love—and so is healed. Bernini's eloquent marble of St. Teresa of Avila in ecstasy in Santa Maria Vittoria in Rome shows a woman lost in rapture, her body pierced with the golden arrow of love—even to her vitals. For God as Designer, Lover and Destiny of our being can, does and will enter our bodies with complete majesty, ardent passion and consummate joy. As St. Augustine says, "God has a passion for us."[20]

A succession of mystics have reacted to God's mystic lovemaking in their commentaries, which are attempts to express feebly the profundity of their mystical union. Unerringly, they chose the Canticle of Canticles,[21] which, if it is anything, is a praise of erotic love, of the ecstasy of delight in embodiedness. No matter their time, language or locale, mystics have flown to the liquid lines of the Canticle to express limpingly but lovingly the only earthly experience resembling their intense union with the Divine Lover.

For the feminist mystic, in particular, whose experiences were so often denigrated or ridiculed by male directors or theologians, the choice of the Canticle is significant, yet revelatory. She discovered in God's lovemaking that the embrace of God's unifying love was not *better* expressed in the act of human love. Human love turned out to be the copy! Mystic, unitive love, the original! And that love was eminently cognitive as well as emotional. The Lover was supreme Teacher as well. To be loved by God was to be enraptured by love, indeed, but also to experience profoundest learning.

The beautiful act of human intercourse, then, is a faint imitation and glorious attempt to mirror the instant union God produces in our bodies and hearts. Made in God's image, we yearn in intercourse to surrender to another person (transcending our small ego) the gift of self: body, mind and spirit. Sexual intercourse is our loving imitation of how God makes love, and thus, supplies for us the analogy; yet it cannot duplicate the totality of God's power to enter completely into our humanity. So, sexual love must be highly respected for its holiness as the attempt to stand as earthly symbol of God's yearning desire for union with our enspirited bodiliness, God's very condominium.

There are contemporary poets who, like the author of the Canticle, praise human sexual love. They are in the direct line of St. John of the Cross, Ramon Lull, author of *Book of the Lover and the Beloved,* and all mystic-poets who sing of union in formal language. William Everson,[22] for example, poetizes the mystical nature of sexual union in his outpouring of erotic poetry. His poetry recognizes *eros,* that love of power, beauty and creativity, in the sexual drive itself as an aspect of all that is deeply human and of our yearning for God. Everson lauds *eros* because in its total pervasion of our lives it is the source of life that fuels our love for divine or human lover.

Certainly the love we experience for God, from God and with God as feminist mystics must happen in a sexual way by dint of the fact that we love embodied. The love of God manifest in our spirituality is influenced and shaped by our sexuality in turn.[23] It can be strengthened or weakened as we accept or reject God's plan in the design of our bodies as female givers and receivers of loving in the dance with God.

God loves each human person uniquely, in a cherishing that is total of body, mind, heart and spirit. Each of us is "someone for God" and God's heart thrills when we, God's beloved, accept that fact and are thrilled with love in turn. Out of such loving encounters comes the wisdom of the spiritual dictum: never imitate slavishly another's spirituality because God is constantly seducing us into accepting our own as the divine vehicle of loving in the world.

Women for centuries have gazed at male models of holiness, and, turning to their daily experience of female sexuality, found it wanting as a vehicle for sanctity. But today, accepting the reality of God's cherishing women as sexual- spiritual individuals, accepting this female identity as God's precious idea, highlights feminist spirituality as a truly valid vehicle for living out our love. At last God's message can come through: "I love you as you are: human, sexual, spiritual, my uniquely precious woman, my beloved."

Women are called to shine back to God and to all about them the incredible experience of being loved by such a One *through* living out sexuality, as well as spirituality, and both together. Even if only in our daily amazement, wondering yearning, joyful expectation and stunned delight at nature's bounteous gifting us with dazzling color, scent and sound, we know the Beloved is near. We, too, see His blood upon the rose, know God in the diamond eye and flashing wing of a bluebird, while the white night awes our timid, quivering souls.

To express that wonder, we need to fulfill, also, our obligation to think through, to philosophize and theologize as women, using our minds to comprehend what is happening to our spirits. Then, using our hearts in prayer and meditation, we listen intently, with our feminist selves, to what God is communicating to us, endowed with sexuality not as problem but as gift, not as evil but as present and pregnant glory.

There are noteworthy precedents for our writing of divine and human loving out of our experiences as women. The remarkable move of the Roman Catholic Church in 1950 (a move praised by C. G. Jung) to state that Mary, Mother of Jesus Christ, was assumed into heaven in *bodily* form was a faint beginning of religious acceptance of the body in our time, even if its authors did not see it as such. Truth has a way of coming home to its authors, and like it or not, this statement implies that the only human body now with God of whose holiness we are *assured* is that of a woman!

Jung saw that delaration as a restoration of the missing feminine element of the Church to its rightful partnership, and so rejoiced. Male Catholics perhaps have not seen that aspect, but as women begin to turn history around to build feminist spiritualities, the significance of such a declaration becomes clear.

Jesus Christ, also, entered history through the mediation of a human body, again, the body of a woman, Mary; hers was the holy of holies for the God-Man. She was his teacher, guide and model, and she failed in none of her tasks. Instead of seeing Mary as some unattainable model in her virginal motherhood, women can relate to her as *the human* who was chosen, a female, to be alone worthy of such intimacy with God-the-Mother's own son.

In Paul's teachings on the body and its members as the

Temples of the Holy Spirit, there is strong support for a feminist mysticism that is eminently social, sexual and spiritual. Paul insists that it is our "bodies" that are such temples; that we are "inhabited" by the lofty God. So also are we "members" one of another (in every way!) Like parts of a body we are called on to love and not reject our bodies, for they image God in our spiritual-sexual members, our organs of relating. To be person is to be in relation, as God, too, is relational, the attribute so well elaborated by St. Augustine in his masterpiece, the *De Trinitate*. As relational, we are sexual, certainly, for as we have seen, we cannot relate except through some power of our embodiedness. By analogy, then, we found God to be sexual and spiritual, but in God's way to constitute those attributes which we mirror. God, then, not only is love; God makes love.

Theology, like the other sciences, is beginning happily to take a humbler stance, to be somewhat less dogmatic about its "knowings." Theologians admit candidly that in some instances they did not quite "know" what they promulgated so clearly some years ago. We now admit, too, that for us, like our fellow scientists, reality may well be a "lost object." Theology will look with great attention to its major premise: We theologize about what we do not "know" — God. So, we may react with fear or shock to changing our concept of God, but change we must as world facts and values impinge on our consciousness and value systems. In the present explosion of theories in theology, we might allow God to return to our world as God chooses to be and not as we assign Her a role. Could s/he be *mysterium tremendum* and still *intimior intimo meo* — closer than our inmost selves?

As we try to make statements in the human effort to convey meaning, we use categories that carry that meaning for people today. We need not thus discard the best of past theory, but rather build upon and judiciously select from it the meaningful items for understanding how God is acting in our world in this time and place.

To change my theology, then, is not to lose my "faith," for faith both precedes and presupposes theology for its interpretation. But theology never created faith, nor do we reason to it; no doctrine created it, for it is belief in, response to, God's touch.

Spirituality grows in its witness to the touch of faith, our theology, and gives it life, for it enables us to live our love. Yet, marvelously enough, each faith-experience, each theology, each spirituality lives within a culture characterized by its language and the uniqueness of the individual lover. So God's touch is experienced artistically as God, the tremendous lover, touches us according to our individual selves.

Always that spirituality of ours is highly conditioned in turn by our image of the God who touches, and so we also respond to that God as we image Her — taught by our community what to call Her. Thus, the immense importance of inclusive language (including the female) in prayer and worship, in the academic forum, in all of political, cultural and public life. If we become what we are told we are, then women must now hear the new word: "You are important; you are man's equal in my sight; you are loved; you are worthy; you are utterly unique; your female embodiedness is my trysting place." Our feminist spirituality needs now to reflect woman's incredible breakthrough in consciousness, opportunity and realization.

So it does make a difference which theology undergirds spirituality, just as it makes a difference which philosophy supports that theology. Today philosophy and theology no longer can operate with the notion of an "essential nature having an existence," the Thomist model fashioned out of Plato and Augustine with Aristotelian nuances. What we experience as humans is ourselves ever in process, constantly transmuting phases of experience, passing into other phases, evolving. Life, in Whitehead's terms, "comes in drops of experience." In such an ambiance, God appears dynamic, changing, moving with us and through us in time and space. This image of God is appropriate to the growing spirituality of the feminist mystic whose self-image will be and is not being shaped upon foundations that will bear the weight of feminist sanctity: the foundations of cherishing sexuality as God's gift. We have said that the mystic is feminist; that, she must be. So too is she sexual. She cannot be otherwise — or she fails her humanity as well as her Designer.

NOTES

1. Daniel D. Williams, *Spirit and Forms of Love* (New York: Harper & Row, 1968), p. 220.

2. E. O. James, *The Cult of the Mother-Goddess* (New York: Doubleday, 1959), p. 180.

3. Tertullian, *De cultu feminarum*, vol. 4; bk. 1 in the Ante-Nicene Fathers.

4. Rosemary Haughton, *Love* (Baltimore: Penguin, 1971), p. 46.

5. Samuel Laeuchli, *Power and Sexuality* (Philadelphia: Temple University Press, 1972, *passim* for a study of the Council of Elvira, a fourth-century assembly that, before Nicaea, began to legislate sexual preference for clerics.

6. Sr. Albertus Magnus McGrath, *Women and the Church* (New York: Image Books, 1976), pp. 17ff.

7. Joan Morris, *The Lady Was a Bishop* (New York: Macmillan, 1973), p. 57.

8. From selections in Elizabeth Clark and Herbert Richardson, *Women and Religion* (New York: Harper & Row, 1977).

9. Peter Berger, *Social Construction of Reality* (New York: Anchor, 1967), Introduction, *passim.*

10. Catherine of Genoa, *Purgation & Purgatory* and *Spiritual Dialogue,* themselves based on the *Vita e Dottrina* published in Genoa by Jacob Geneti in 1551, itself perhaps due to Don Cattaneo Marabotto, her spiritual director. Benedict Groeschel's fine introduction in the Paulist Press Classics of Western Spirituality Series should be read.

11. Anders Nygren, *Agape and Eros* (London: SPCK, 1957), p. 75 ff.

12. Rollo May, *Love and Will* (New York: Norton, 1969), p. 40.

13. James B. Nelson, *Embodiment* (Minneapolis, Augsburg, 1978), p. 113.

14. Jules Toner, SJ, *What is Love?* (Washington, D.C., Corpus, 1968), p. 41 ff.

15. Sebastian Moore, "Love and Theology," an unpublished paper, 1979.

16. St. Teresa of Avila, *Meditations on the Song of Songs,* trans. Otilio Rodriguez and Kieran Kavanaugh, Vol. II: *The Collected Works of St. Teresa of Avila* (Washington, D.C., Carmelites Studies, 1980), Ch. 2, 3, and 4.

17. Hadewijch of Brabant, Letter 18 in *The Complete Works,* trans. Mother Columba Hart, OSB, *Classics of Western Spirituality* (Ramsey, N.J.: Paulist Press, 1980).

18. St. John of the Cross, "The Dark Night," preface to *Ascent of Mount Carmel,* vv. 35-40. The commentary and translation of Kieran Kavanaugh and Otilio Rodriguez are particularly fine in the Carmelite Studies (Washington, D.C.) 1979 edition of the *Collected Works of St. John of the Cross.*

19. Michel de Certeau, SJ, "Mysticisme" in the *French Encyclopedia Universalis,* Paris.

20. St. Augustine of Hippo, *Tractatus in Joannis evangelium,* this sentiment is expressed *passim* by the older Augustine; see Homilies on the Gospel according to St. John (2 vols) Oxford, 1848.

21. The Anchor Bible volume of the Canticle of Canticles with its voluminous notes would be a fruitful study for references to all those mystics and theologians who found expression for their experience in the lines of the Canticle.

22. William Everson (formerly Brother Antoninus), "River Root Syzygy" (Oyez Press, California, 1976).

23. Many of the ideas in this essay originate in Dody H. Donnelly's newly completed manuscript, *Sex and Spirit,* a theology of integration.

CHAPTER 7

Armed with a Burning Patience: Reflections on Simone Weil

🍎 *Kathyrn Hohlwein*

Visionary though he was, the adolescent nineteenth-century poet Arthur Rimbaud could not foretell the variants on his vision, nor the terms of its realization. Toward the end of his tortured *A Season In Hell* he said, "At dawn, armed with a burning patience, we shall enter the splendid cities." We are accustomed to being reminded, by many great and lesser minds of this century, that, as Heidegger says, "It is still not dawn." We are in dark times, in desperate times. The nature and degree of the darkness continues to be defined, but most of us have lived into our own acquaintance with the desolation, even if only by our flailing around in a struggle *not* to admit its existence. "The only way not to suffer is to lapse into unconsciousness; and there are many who yield, in one way or another, to this temptation. . . . To retain the lucidity, self-responsibility, and dignity appropriate to a human being . . . means condemning oneself to a renewed fight every day against despair."[1] It is not yet DAWN. We do not yet know the splendid cities. If Rimbaud was truly a visionary, as the great poet Pablo Neruda acclaimed him to be in his Nobel Prize acceptance speech, if there really is (yet) to be a beneficent turning around from our modern flight from the divine, we do not know how to do it. Angelic as Rimbaud was capable of being, he once had the "illumination" that our turning would be "as simple as a musical phrase." But we do not yet know how to hear it.

Almost a century later, a tortured compatriate of Rimbaud, Simone Weil, struggled with her immense spiritual gifts as uniquely as he had done. Both had enormous capacities for solitude and inwardness such as most of us cannot emulate nor comprehend. Both were idiosyncratic, puzzling, and each remains difficult to approach, resistant to simplification, explication, criticism. They leave us wondering. Believers without structures, both had an ambiguous relationship to traditional Christianity, both have been considered mystics, and both cultivated *attention* as a spiritual method. Both were, finally, "God-intoxicated" and lovers of truth. We are learning to approach them.

It is not my intention in this essay to further compare Rimbaud with Simone Weil, although I think it should be done. Rather, I believe that her clumsy but pure life somehow embodies Rimbaud's prophetic outcry—that he, at some level, perhaps had one such as she in mind.

It is appropriate that the quote does not isolate *one* who enters. Rather, it is *we* who shall enter the splendid cities. Simone Weil, despite her uniqueness and because of it, knew herself to be born for a "fellowship in love." Whether we consider her a crank, a masochist, or a saint, we *must* acknowledge her need to *act* upon her compassion—always. Her need and ability to be alone only intensified her ache for service, to the point of self-abnegation, to self-inflicted starvation.

She might have appeared just as she did in her last photographs, with her worn sandals and anarchist's beret—at any gathering of the oppressed—in Nicaragua, in El Salvador, as a spokesperson for Solidarity in Poland. Like Joe Hill, Simone Weil is there whenever there is a gathering of the oppressed. Always her effort was to ask how human rights could be realized, human misery lessened, human labor made bearable, human dignity preserved.

> The suffering all over the world obsesses and overwhelms me to the point of annihilating my faculties and the only way I can revive them and release myself from the obsession is by getting for myself a large share of danger and hardship. That is a necessary condition before I exert my capacity for work.[2]

Despite the hardships such a conviction imposed upon a frail woman, finally, at the end of her life, dying in a sanatorium in England, she could write that

> I too have a growing inner certainty that there is within me a deposit of pure gold, which must be handed on [and that despite the feeling that] there is no one to receive it, [that] before there is a generation with muscle and power of thought the books and manuscripts of our day will surely have disappeared [that, nonetheless,] the mine of gold is inexhaustible.[3]

The splendid city, the civilization that we cannot foresee, for Simone Weil would have been a more humane order carried forward into realization by those capable of *attention*, those who could resist the "gravity," the down-drag of this world, by a spirit of patient *waiting*, which can allow *grace* to enter. "The problem is to raise oneself in this life to the level of eternal things."[4]

Despising war with a passion that glows fiercely in her magnificent and famous essay — "The Iliad or the Poem of Force" — Simone Weil nonetheless finally and painfully abandoned her pacifist position when Hitler invaded Prague in May, 1939. But all her life she was to grapple with paradox, struggle to identify the *lesser* evil, so as to know how to be *armed*, as Rimbaud so militarily puts it. Her answer was his. Above all she would arm with patience, but an almost violent, vigilant patience, indeed, a burning patience.

Now what this means in her case requires a look at her history. Simone Weil was born in Paris in 1909. Her family were assimilated Jews, and her father a prosperous doctor. The assimilation was so total that, to the end, she considered her heritage to be French, Christian and Greek, and one of her most infuriating insistencies is her prejudicial reading of her own Jewish tradition. Brought up as an agnostic, a rationalist, she scarcely knew that she was a Jew. She was well cared for and loved by her parents, to whom she was always an enigma, but she felt hopelessly inferior to her brother, André, who was as a child a genius in mathematics. She was a gorgeous little girl, and friends of the family remarked that in the Weil family, one child had genius, the other, beauty. It is astonishing to compare her early portraits with the few that we have of her as a very plain woman. One thinks that it must have taken a will to self-destruction. What we know about her early life strikes us as amazingly consistent with her life as she was to lead it. At the age of five, in 1914, she refused sugar because the men at the front were denied it. The kind of injunctions all of us heard while growing up — to clear our plates because of the starving children in India — she took seriously, so seriously that she not only cleared her plate in deference to human situations less well-favored than her own —

she simply didn't put the food on the plate at all. Also at five, and more deliberately at fourteen, she trained herself to fix her attention on things — anything — for extended periods of time. Later, in some of her finest passages, she was to think very deeply on *attention*; it was to become her spiritual method. She was a child who did not cry and seemed a born stoic; later she was to denounce all forms of "consolation," all that might fill up the void so that "grace" could not enter. During adolescence she began to suffer from the migraine headaches that tortured her all her life, which were to reduce her at times to a quivering heap of pain. Again, in her mature writings, "suffering" was to become for her indispensable to spiritual growth.

Self-critical to a fault, she was nonetheless very impressive to others. No one who met her doubted her brilliance. She unwittingly intimidated others by her depth, and had a compelling strength that forced people to acknowledge her ideas. Her famous philosophy teacher, "Alain," recognized her mind as one of unusual power. As a young student, she was already a radical and a revolutionary, already attracted to trade unionism, already concerning herself with the nature of the social, already distressed that society resists the spirit — the spirit resists society. These preoccupations were to last all her life. In 1928, she tested first for admission to the École Normale, winning over Simone de Beauvoir, who placed second, both far outflanking the male applicants. Again her professors considered her eccentric, *too* original, but recognized the indomitable courage and fierce loyalty to truth. There was something luminous about her. Simone de Beauvoir wrote that she "envied her for having a heart that could beat right across the world."[5]

In spite of her growing radicalism and commitment to social action, Simone was studying philosophy, Greek, science, and especially mathematics; these sources of her erudition were to serve as bases for analogies all her life, and her last notebooks are full of mathematical models and discussions of Euclid and Pythagoras as well as of Plato and the Gospels.

Her first job was teaching philosophy at Le Puy, where she impressed her students, worried their parents, and forced the administrators to keep a close eye on her. She taught them with an educative genius so original that many of her girl students flunked the Baccalaureate. But the plight of the unemployed of Le Puy concerned her more than satisfying school administrators did. She disliked being a paid teacher in the midst of unemployment. Though she was outside union discipline, she urged the workers at Le Puy to strike, and the mayor gave orders that she be watched. She felt that it was not enough to revolt against a social order founded on oppression, that one had to change it and that one could not change it without understanding it. Her first writings were almost all concerned with the nature of labor. She wanted to establish the workers' control over the processes of work, was keenly aware of the degrading division between intellectual work and manual labor. She had the kind of heroic dedication to the poor of Le Puy that one thinks of with Van Gogh and his potato eaters. She spent most of her time with the working class, gave most of her salary away to them, and fully perplexed them. She irritated the school administrators and was in no way intimidated when they threatened her dismissal.

In 1933, at Auxerre, people continued to consider her a crank and a troublemaker, and a Communist, which she was not. She was tough, an ardent pacifist at first, as well as a defender of the individual against the state. She wrote of her fear of Russian bureaucracy. Administrators began snooping in her students' notebooks to see how subversive their teacher really was and encountered her characteristic thinking. "A wife is a mistress reduced to slavery." "Emotion, associations and language operate through the mediation of the imagination. The only remedy is doubt." "However little suffering remains it will be of first importance to relieve it." "The only thing of value is to make evident the rights of man."[6]

Throughout the thirties, Simone Weil's own idea of the revolution was being shaped. She kept rephrasing ideas about the necessity of subordinating society to the individual. She took to task the Stalinist States and feared a cult of the state. At the Trade Union Congress at Rheims, in courageous speeches from the floor, she dealt with the unmentionable — the collusion between Hitler and Stalin. They were dangerous sentiments, and the miners she had fought for protected her. She was condemning both the Communist party and German facism — and simultaneously raising funds for anti-fascist German refugees, and she kept insisting that the individual is the only true lever of revolution.

Feeling strongly a growing need to really know working-class life, she took a leave of absence disguised as a vacation and went to work for a year in a Renault factory near Paris. She was frequently ill with migraine headaches and the effort to work at mechanized labor while fighting pain was hard on her already frail health. The *meaning* of mechanization was what she sought to know, and she wrote impassioned letters to industrial managers, urging them to realize what a worker's life was like, urging them to reform, to help. She was asking of herself the same question Solzhenitzyn asks in *One Day in the Life of Ivan Denisovich* — how to preserve human dignity. The work taught her that slavery as both a physical and a spiritual condition was as widespread in the modern as in the ancient world, and she regarded herself as a slave. How, she was to ask over and over, can society be organized so that suffering shall be reduced and dignity maintained, and how can it be ensured that the irreducible minimum of suffering that necessarily would remain might have *some* value?

Throughout these years of political activism and zeal for the proletarian revolution, Simone Weil continued her vast studies in geometry, comparative religion, folklore, Sanskrit, and Greek studies of all kinds. The profundity of her love for the Greeks never left her. In 1940, she wrote to André:

> The Greeks attached no value to a method of reasoning for its own sake, they valued it in so far as it enabled concrete problems to be studied efficiently. And this was not because they were avid for technical applications but because their sole aim was to conceive more and more clearly an identity of structure between the human mind and the universe. Purity of soul was their one concern; to "imitate God" was the secret of it; the imitation of God was assisted by the study of mathematics, in so far as one conceived the universe to be subject to mathematical laws, which made the geometer an imitator of the supreme law giver.[7]

and

> True, the Greek conception of existence was a sad one, as it is for all whose eyes are open; but their sadness had a motive; it had meaning *in relation to* the happiness for which man is made and of which he is deprived by the harsh constraints of this world. They had no taste for affliction, disaster, disequilibrium. Whereas there are so many modern people (and notably Nietzche, I believe) in whom sadness is connected with a loss of the very instinct for happiness; they feel a need to

annihilate themselves. In my opinion there is no
anguish in the Greeks. That is what makes them dear to
me. In struggling against anguish one never produces
serenity; the struggle against anguish only produces
new forms of anguish. But the Greeks possessed grace
from the beginning.[8]

Simone Weil's thought was richly indebted to Greek
thought, but also to comparative religions and to folklore.
She was a syncretist who believed that

one single thought is to be found — expressed very precisely and with only very slight differences of modality in
the ancient mythologies; in the philosophies of Phereky-
des, Thales, Anaximander, Heraclitus, Pythagoras, Plato, and the Greek Stoics; in Greek poetry of the great
age, in universal folklore; in the *Upanishads* and the
Bhagavad-Gita; in the Chinese Taoist writings and in
certain currents of Buddhism; in what remains of the
sacred writings of the greatest Christian mystics, especially St. John of the Cross, and in certain heresies, especially the Cathar and Manichaean tradition. I believe
that this thought is the truth, and that it requires today a
modern and Western form of expression.[9]

During most of this time she spoke of Christ in a way that
did not suggest her susceptibility to his love. But her thought
begins to dwell on human limitation, on illusion, on the
meaning of obedience. Her social preoccupations still shaped
her activities, she still gave her salary away and began to pay
less and less attention to what she ate or how she looked, and
her notebooks begin to reveal the directions of her later books
— *Waiting for God* and *Gravity and Grace*.

In her intellectual development, she had always been willing to doubt. She had even described her method of investi-

gation as one of immediately searching out any truth in the contrary of a fixed position. Likewise in her spiritual inquiries. Like Pascal, with whom she is often compared, her thought proceeded by paradox, and her theology was one of tension. "I see nothing to be shocked at in the fact that one has to refer to two incompatible images in order to give an account of a phenomenon — for images never do more than represent analogies in a manner 'acceptable to the heart,' as Pascal would say."[10] Still, this struggle with doubt wore on her and late in her short life she wrote to her friend, Maurice Schummann:

> I feel an ever increasing sense of devastation, both in my intellect and in the centre of my heart, at my inability to think *with truth* [emphasis mine] at the same time about the affliction of men, the perfection of God, and the link between the two.[11]

The Spanish Civil War seriously engaged her commitment and finally resulted in disillusion. She saw evil on both sides. And from these painful revelations she began to believe in redemptive suffering. It was clear to her that

> . . . in an absurd world contradiction is the criterion of reality. To be innocent is to bear the weight of the whole universe. It is to throw in the counterweight to restore the balance. . . . Equilibrium alone reduces force to nothing. If we know in what way society is unbalanced, we must do what we can to add weight to the lighter scale. Although the weight may consist of evil, in handling it with this intention, perhaps we do not become defiled. But we must have formed a conception of equilibrium and be ever ready to change sides like justice, that fugitive from the camp of conquerors.[12]

Always she was concerned, as was Martin Buber, with the

reduction of people to things, and she was very alert to the arrogance of colonialism. She began publishing articles against French policy in Morocco, ironically accusing the Popular Front administration of feeling that the gravity of injustice diminishes in proportion to distance. After all, they were natives; they were a species apart. They were accustomed to suffering. All the little ten- or twelve-year-olds who were starving and overworked, who perished of exhaustion in the mines of Indochina, had died without bloodshed. Such deaths did not count, they were not real deaths. For the bourgeois, social issues only begin to matter when they give rise to news sensational enough to displace crime from the front page. Because of such sarcasm and outspokenness, first on the nature of the Spanish Civil War and then on colonialism, Simone Weil became controversial, was praised or ridiculed, and was also called a saint. It seems that our time is intrigued by what we consider excessive and extreme, almost irrespective of whether we attribute the excess to sanctity or to sickness, and it thus happened that her pathetic figure was glamorized, sensationalized.

So we return to the perplexity of Simone Weil. Who was she? Powerful as she is, it is not easy to make contact with this often unsympathetic loner, this paradox of a genius. Her overwhelming erudition, her extreme statements which sometimes infuriate, sometimes vitiate her writing, her difficult jumble of comparative mythology, politics, Eastern wisdom and bodily pain against which she defined her vision—all conspire to make us feel that "approaching Simone" is almost too hard, that she is too ahead of us to approach, that she is too severe for us to *want* to approach. Was she a mystic? A revolutionary? A feminist? A saint? She was, I believe, a genius, a bridge, but to what we do not yet know.

How could anyone be both a mystic and an activist, a critic of patriotism who died from sympathy for her compatriots in Vichy France, a supporter of "the need for roots" who has been called the "outsider as saint," a Catholic who refused to be baptised, a member of the radical left who spoke out against Communism, and a Jew who hated what she felt to be the tyranny inherent in Judaism, and still come out all of one piece, even though an odd piece? Was she, as Leslie Fiedler once suggested, a Holy Fool? Withal, she was wonderful.

In 1938, she had the major religious experience of her life, during the Easter services at the Abbaye of Solesmes. Her only written expression about her experience was very simply stated, in a letter to her friend, Joe Posquet. "I enclose the English poem, "Love", which I recited to you. It has played a big role in my life, because I was repeating it to myself at the moment when Christ came to take possession of me for the first time. I thought I was only reciting a beautiful poem, but, unknown to me, it was a prayer."[13] The event had astonished her. In a talk with Father Perrin, she later said that she considered it God's mercy that she had been prevented from reading the mystics, so that she could feel this presence of love, this sudden possession by Christ, with no sense of preparation. It was for her a totally unexpected contact.

From this point on she was increasingly concerned, if not obsessed, with mysticism, with Catholicism, with her speculation on what she calls Gravity and its opposite, Grace, and with her theories of attention, with her own self-denial and suffering. There is a formidable opposition to her by those people who find such otherwordly concern unbefitting a radical, by her orthodox friends who were dismayed at her refusal to be baptised, by those who give her the quick psychological overhaul and find her uncongenial, often described as the classic neurotic female — absurd in her excesses. But now, some decades later, more and more people end up honoring her for the integrity and purity of her spirituality. And hers was not a conversion that canceled earlier passions. She never ceased to be a revolutionary. She was the eternal radical.

There is, for those of us torn as she was between contemplation and social action, a comfort and an encouragement in her conviction that a contemplation of the social scene can be a form of purification, which is as effective as a withdrawal from the world. She was never comfortable with the idea of herself as a mystic, claimed that she didn't understand mystical phenomena, but knew that the great task was to transform daily life somehow into a parable, to make it a metaphor of divine significance. She considered love not a condition. Rather it was a direction. The soul of genius was "caritas."[14]

A quote from Gustave Thibon, a wealthy Catholic farmer who allowed her to work his vineyards, gives us an unforgettable final portrait of this woman.

> She was just then beginning to open with all her soul to Christianity; a limpid mysticism emanated from her; in no other human being have I come across much familiarity with religious mysteries; never have I felt the word supernatural to be more charged with reality than when in contact with her.
>
> Such mysticism had nothing in common with those religious speculations divorced from any personal commitment which are all too frequently the only testimony of intellectuals who apply themselves to the things of God. She actually experienced in its heartbreaking reality the distance between knowing and knowing with all one's soul, and the one object of her life was to abolish that distance. I have witnessed too much of the daily unfolding of her existence to be left

with the slightest doubt of the authenticity of her spiritual vocation; her faith and detachment were expressed in all her actions, sometimes with a disconcerting disregard for the practical but always with absolute generosity.

and

I will simply say that I had the feeling of being in the presence of a creature utterly transparent, ready almost to be absorbed again into the primal light. Her words did not so much translate the truth as pour it into me whole and unadulterated. I felt as if I were being transported beyond space and time, so that I virtually fed upon the light. The nature of her humility and love is such that she appears as pure messenger. I have never ceased to believe in her.[15]

Simone Weil may or may not represent the kind of messenger that Rimbaud seemed to be suggesting. Her life does not seem as "simple as a musical phrase." But there is a unity in her vision, and a great patience in her affliction. Close upon her death, she wrote to Joe Bosquet:

You have only a thin shell to break before emerging from the darkness inside the egg into the light of truth. It is a very ancient image. The egg is this world we see. The bird in it is Love, the Love which is God himself and which lives in the depths of every man, though at first an invisible seed. When the shell is broken and the being is released, it still has this same world before it. But it is no longer inside. Space is opened and torn apart. The spirit, leaving the miserable body in some corner, is transported to a point outside space, which is not a point of view, which has no perspective, but from which this world is seen as it is, unconfused by perspective. Compared to what is inside the egg, space has become an infinite to the second or rather the third power. The moment stands still. The whole of space is filled, even though sounds can be heard, with a dense silence which is not an absence of sound but is a positive object of sensation; it is the secret word of Love which holds us in his arms from the beginning.

. . . . Thanks to the immobility [of affliction] the infinitesimal seed of divine love placed in the soul can slowly grow and bear fruit in patience. The divinely beautiful Gospel expression means to remain where one is, motionless, in expectation, unshaken and unmoved by any external shock.[16]

Simone Weil went to England, where she was to die. Ill and alone she wrote her most well-known book, *The Need For Roots.* Her death made clear the awesome sincerity with which she had conceived this book and subtitled it *Prelude to a Declaration of Duties Toward Mankind.* The book reads simply. At the heart of it is the piercing conviction that modern man is rootless because he has lost contact with the divinity of the world itself. It was a book the effect of which, T. S. Eliot said, would become apparent in the attitude of mind of another generation.[17]

Love was a direction of the heart with Simone Weil. Lonely, afflicted and alone, her longings were for the joy and dignity of others, and she bore with heroic patience and charity her vision of a grace that was possible for all human beings.

NOTES

1. Richard Rees, ed., *Seventy Letters* (New York: Oxford University Press, 1965), p. 57.

2. *Ibid.*, p. 156.

3. *Ibid.*, pp. 196–197.

4. *Ibid.*, p. 87.

5. Simone Petrement, *Simone Weil, A Life*, translated from the French by Raymond Rosenthal (New York: Pantheon Books, 1971), p. 51.

6. J. B. Perrin and G. Thibon, *Simone Weil As We Knew Her*, (London: Routledge and Kegan Paul, 1953), p. 113.

7. *Seventy Letters*, pp. 117–118.

8. *Ibid.*, p. 123.

9. *Ibid.*, p. 159.

10. *Ibid.*, p. 89.

11. *Ibid.*, p. 178.

12. Emma Crawford, trans., *Gravity and Grace* (London: Routledge and Kegan Paul, 1952), Introduction.

13. *Seventy Letters*, p. 142.

14. *Ibid.*, p. 104.

15. *Gravity and Grace*, Introduction.

16. *Seventy Letters*, pp. 136–137.

17. Arthur Wills, trans., *The Need For Roots*, with a preface by T. S. Eliot (New York: G. P. Putnam's Sons, 1952), Preface.

About the Authors

Mary E. Giles, Professor of Humanities and Religious Studies at California State University, Sacramento, is founding editor of *Studia Mystica*, a quarterly journal of mysticism and the arts. She is the author of many articles on Spanish literature and spirituality and translated Francisco de Osuna's *Third Spiritual Alphabet* for the Classics of Western Spirituality series, published by Paulist Press. She also teaches seminars and gives retreats on prayer and spirituality.

Meinrad Craighead, artist and poet, has lived in Europe since 1962 and for fourteen years was a nun in an English Benedictine monastic community. Educated in Vienna, Austria and the United States, she has taught art and art history at various universities and institutes, including Schifanoia Institute of Fine Arts, Florence, Italy. Two books of her poetry, essays and paintings were published in 1975 and 1979 and she has illustrated three books. She is currently working on the imagery and text for another book, *The Mother*, from which portions of her essay here are taken.

Margaret R. Miles is Associate Professor of Historical Theology at the Harvard Graduate Divinity School, having earned the Ph.D. from the Graduate Theological Union, Berkeley,

California. She writes and lectures extensively on Western mysticism, and her book, *Fullness of Life*, was published in 1981.

Wendy M. Wright, a doctoral candidate in an interdisciplinary program in Contemplative Studies at the University of California, Santa Barbara, has been doing special research in the Archive Library at the Monastery of the Visitation in Annecy, France. She is coauthor of *Silent Fire: An Invitation to Western Mysticism*.

Dorothy H. Donnelly, who holds the Ph.D. from Catholic University of America and the Th.D. from the Graduate Theological Union, Berkeley, has taught and lectured widely. Her many publications include *Team* (Paulist Press, 1977) and articles in the *National Catholic Reporter, Commonweal* and the *National Catholic Encyclopedia*. Her ongoing interest in prison reform and women has spurred formation of an organization, *Women Today-West*.

Kathryn Hohlwein, Professor of Humanities and English at California State University, Sacramento, is Art & Poetry editor for *Studia Mystica*. A much published poet, she gives numerous poetry readings, and her book, *Touchstones*, appears through Harper & Row in 1982.